The High School Athlete's Guide to College Sports

The
High School Athlete's
Guide to College Sports

How to Market Yourself
to the School of Your Dreams

COLLEGE BOUND SPORTS

TAYLOR TRADE PUBLISHING
Lanham • New York • Dallas • Boulder • Toronto • Oxford

Published by Taylor Trade Publishing
An imprint of The Rowman & Littlefield Publishing Group, Inc.
4501 Forbes Boulevard, Suite 200
Lanham, Maryland 20706

Distributed by National Book Network

Library of Congress Cataloging-in-Publication Data

The high school athlete's guide to college sports.
    p. cm.
  Includes bibliographical references.
  ISBN 1-58979-192-4 (pbk. : alk. paper)
    1. College athletes—Recruiting—United States. 2. College sports—United States.
  3. College choice—United States. I. College Bound Sports (Organization)
  GV350.5.H55 2005   2004026817

♾™ The paper used in this publication meets the minimum requirements of American National Standard for Information Sciences—Permanence of Paper for Printed Library Materials, ANSI/NISO Z39.48–1992.
Manufactured in the United States of America.

Get Recruited!

Acknowledgments

We would like to thank all of the college coaches, high school coaches, pro scouts, guidance counselors, and college admissions officers who have contributed information for this guide. Excerpts from *U.S. News & World Report* articles and NCAA, NAIA, and NJCAA literature are also incorporated.

Every effort has been made to make this guide as accurate as possible. Nevertheless, you should still contact the appropriate college organizations, since rules and requirements change frequently. College Bound Sports cannot assume responsibility for any errors contained herein.

We Want to Hear from You!

Please e-mail any additions, corrections, ideas, or personal stories that you feel would improve this guide to info@collegeboundsports.com.

What Coaches Are Saying

"An extremely valuable tool for high school baseball athletes. I strongly recommend it to any athlete who aspires to play college sports."
Chip Baker, Assistant Baseball Coach, Florida State University

"The recruiting process can be confusing and clouded by misconceptions. This guide is very informative and a realistic tool for guiding a prospect in the right direction. . . . A quality resource!"
Scot Thomas, Head Softball Coach, Virginia Tech University

"This guide can be extremely valuable if it gets into the right hands. High school athletes should definitely take advantage of what it offers."
Dan Ireland, Head Cross-Country Coach, Yale University (CT)

"A guide like this teaches athletes how to be proactive and how to organize an effective approach to the college recruiting process."
Amy Bartlett, Assistant Field Hockey Coach, Bryant College (RI)

"The more information an athlete has, the more equipped he or she will be to make a better choice for college. *The High School Athlete's Guide to College Sports* fits that category."
Matt Centrowitz, Head Track and Field Coach, American University (DC)

"This helps the students to do the most thorough research possible. It helps them be the best equipped and to be the best prepared to compete at the collegiate level."

Dermon Player, Assistant Basketball Coach, St. John's University (NY)

"Deciding where to compete, learn, and live for four years is a difficult decision. A guide like this is a perfect investment for someone in need of direction."

Ben DeLuca, Assistant Lacrosse Coach, Cornell University (NY)

"The recruiting process can be one of the most enjoyable experiences in life, and yet it can be one of the most painful. This guide will give both athlete and parent a better feeling of doing the right thing when it comes to starting the process and its eventual conclusion."

Lance Harter, Head Women's Track Coach, University of Arkansas

"This guide gives you the opportunity to choose the correct school to fit all your needs, so when your athletic career is over, you are well prepared to lead a productive life."

Raphael Cerrato, Assistant Baseball Coach and Recruiting Coordinator, Brown University (RI)

"A must-buy for any aspiring college athlete."

Bill Edwards, Head Softball Coach, Hofstra University (NY)

"A great tool for high school student-athletes and their parents. There is a lot of critical information given with an emphasis on academic considerations."

Ken Browning, Football Recruiting Coordinator, University of North Carolina

Advisors

We would like to thank the following people in the sports community for contributing valuable information to the guide and supporting our effort to help high school athletes navigate the college recruiting maze.

Organization	Advisor	Current or Former Title
ABILENE CHRISTIAN UNIVERSITY (TX)	Jon Murray	Head Coach
AMERICAN UNIVERSITY (DC)	Matt Centrowitz	Head Coach
BASEBALL FACTORY (MD)	Steve Sclafani	CEO
BOSTON COLLEGE (MA)	John Mortimer	Assistant Coach
BOSTON UNIVERSITY (MA)	Amy Hayes	Head Coach
BROCAW BLAZERS CROSS COUNTRY CAMP	John Ramsey	Director
BROWN UNIVERSITY (RI)	Raphael Cerrato	Assistant Coach
BRYANT COLLEGE (RI)	Amy Bartlett	Assistant Coach
CALIFORNIA STATE UNIVERSITY	Cregg Weinmann	Head Coach
CALVIN COLLEGE (MI)	Gary West	Assistant Coach
CINCINNATI REDS	Jim Grief	Pro Scout
CLEVELAND INDIANS	Vic Power	Former 7x All-Star 1B
COAST TO COAST ATHLETICS (OH)	Kevin Ritter	Executive Director
COCOA EXPO SPORTS CENTER (FL)	Jeff Biddle	Director of Athletics
COLLEGE OF CHARLESTON (SC)	Gregg Mucerino	Assistant Coach
COLLEGE OF NEW JERSEY	Dean Glus	Assistant Coach

Organization	Advisor	Current or Former Title
CORNELL UNIVERSITY (NY)	Lou Deusing	Head Coach
CORNELL UNIVERSITY (NY)	Ben DeLuca	Assistant Coach
CORNELL UNIVERSITY (NY)	Dick Blood	Head Coach
DECKER SPORTS USA (NE)	Thomas Decker	President
ELMHURST COLLEGE (IL)	Clark Jones	Head Coach
ELON COLLEGE (NC)	Mike Kennedy	Head Coach
FLORIDA ATLANTIC UNIVERSITY	Bob Deutschman	Assistant Coach
FLORIDA STATE UNIVERSITY	Chip Baker	Assistant Coach
FOCUSED BASEBALL (FL)	Tom Hansen	President
FROZEN ROPES TRAINING CENTER (NY)	Tony Abbatine	President
HIGH PERFORMANCE DISTANCE ACADEMY (VA)	James DeMarco	Director
HIGH SCHOOL SPORTS NETWORK (PA)	Adam Stanco	Producer/Host
HOFSTRA UNIVERSITY (NY)	Mike Reid	Assistant Coach
HOFSTRA UNIVERSITY (NY)	Bill Edwards	Head Coach
HOFSTRA UNIVERSITY (NY)	Larissa Smith	Assistant Coach
HOPE COLLEGE (MI)	Stu Fritz	Head Coach
JOE ESPINOSA BASEBALL SCHOOL (CT)	Joe Espinosa	President
KEENE STATE COLLEGE (NH)	Peter Thomas	Head Coach
LEMOYNE COLLEGE (NY)	Joe Hannah	Head Coach
LONG ISLAND UNIVERSITY (NY)	Roy Kartmann	Head Coach
LOUISIANA STATE UNIVERSITY	Bob Smith	Assistant Coach
MIAMI UNIVERSITY (OH)	Bill Consiglio	Assistant Coach
MICKEY OWEN BASEBALL SCHOOL (MO)	Ken Rizzo	Director
MIKE EPSTEIN HITTING (CA)	Mike Epstein	President/Former MLB Player
MORRIS BROWN COLLEGE (GA)	Marqus Johnson	Assistant Coach
MUHLENBERG COLLEGE (PA)	Ruth Gibbs	Head Coach
NEDCO SPORTS (AL)	Nick Dixon	President
NORTHERN ILLINOIS UNIVERSITY	Donna Martin	Head Coach
NOTRE DAME UNIVERSITY (IN)	Tim Connelly	Head Coach
PADUCAH COMMUNITY COLLEGE (KY)	Rick Tippin	Head Coach
PENSACOLA JUNIOR COLLEGE (FL)	Bill Hamilton	Head Coach
PERKIOMEN SCHOOL (PA)	Kendall Baker	AD/Head Coach
PRESBYTERIAN UNIVERSITY (SC)	Jeremy Farber	Assistant Coach

Organization	Advisor	Current or Former Title
PUERTO RICO BASEBALL ACADEMY	Edwin Correa	President/Former MLB Player
SACRED HEART UNIVERSITY (CT)	Seth Kaplan	Assistant Coach
SAGINAW VALLEY STATE UNIVERSITY (MI)	Fred Neering	Head Coach
SAINT PETER'S COLLEGE (NJ)	Tom Besser	Former Head Coach
SAN JACINTO COLLEGE (TX)	Rob Penders	Assistant Coach
SHIPPENSBURG UNIVERSITY (PA)	Steve Spence	Head Coach/Olympian
SOUTH GEORGIA COLLEGE	Zach Walker	Assistant Coach
SOUTHERN ILLINOIS UNIVERSITY	Dan Callahan	Head Coach
SOUTHWEST HIGH SCHOOL (FL)	Javier Perez	Head Coach
SPRINGFIELD COLLEGE (IL)	Steve Torricelli	Head Coach/Athletic Director
ST. JOHN'S UNIVERSITY (NY)	Dermon Player	Assistant Coach
ST. THOMAS UNIVERSITY (FL)	Manny Mantrana	Head Coach
STANFORD UNIVERSITY (CA)	Dean Stotz	Associate Head Coach
STANFORD UNIVERSITY (CA)	Lonni Alameda	Associate Head Coach
SYRACUSE UNIVERSITY (NY)	Mary J. Firnbach	Head Coach
TENNESSEE TECH UNIVERSITY	Pat Portugal	Assistant Coach
TEXAS A & M UNIVERSITY	Jorge Hernandez	Assistant Coach
TODAY'S MVP.COM (NJ)	Lou Santangelo	CEO
UNITED SOCCER ACADEMY	Bill Fisher	President
UNITED STATES MILITARY ACADEMY (NY)	Michelle Gerdes	Assistant Coach
UNIVERSITY OF ALABAMA	Bobby Pierce	Head Coach
UNIVERSITY OF ARKANSAS	Lance Harter	Head Coach
UNIVERSITY OF CONNECTICUT	Jim Penders	Assistant Coach
UNIVERSITY OF EVANSVILLE (IL)	Al Lopez	Assistant Coach
UNIVERSITY OF NEBRASKA	Ron Wolforth	Assistant Coach
UNIVERSITY OF NORTHERN COLORADO	Terry Hensley	Head Coach
UNIVERSITY OF SOUTH FLORIDA	Bryan Peters	Assistant Coach
UNIVERSITY OF SOUTHERN MISSISSIPPI	Clay Smith	Assistant Coach
VANDERBILT UNIVERSITY (TN)	Derek Johnson	Assistant Coach
VILLANOVA UNIVERSITY (PA)	M. O'Sullivan	Head Coach
VIRGINIA TECH UNIVERSITY (VA)	Scot Thomas	Head Coach
WEST CHESTER UNIVERSITY (PA)	Chris Calciano	Head Coach
YALE UNIVERSITY (CT)	Dan Ireland	Head Coach

Contents

Introduction

Congratulations!

By reading this guide, you are giving yourself an enormous advantage over your competitors—thousands of other high school athletes your age who also want to play college sports.

Gaining admission to the college of your choice can be a daunting experience for the average high school student. The task is even more intricate for athletes. Success requires a solid plan, attention to detail, and disciplined execution. Unfortunately, many high school athletes who are looking to continue competing in college do not have a true understanding of how the recruiting process works, and they never reach their athletic or academic potential.

Because athletic programs often change—old coaches leave, new ones arrive, school and athletic programs change their focus and adapt to rule changes—it is important to have the most current information available in your search for the school that meets your athletic and academic needs. This 2005 edition provides just that.

This book provides a road map for you to follow when making the jump from high school to college sports. If you avoid the mistakes most high school athletes make, if you promote yourself aggressively, and if you improve your athletic and academic skills, we are confident you will find a school that is right for you!

What We Want to Accomplish

Our goal is to help you find a college where you will be able to do the following:

- Receive a good education so that you are well prepared for life after college, whether it includes athletics or not
- Compete on a college team as a starter or role player
- Possibly earn an athletic or academic scholarship
- Obtain the best financial aid package to lower the expenses of college for you and your family
- Feel confident in your ultimate college selection, reducing the chance of transferring or dropping out

A Big Decision

We hope you're excited about the opportunity that awaits you: the chance to attend college and continue your sports career. College promises to be one of the most enjoyable, rewarding, and memorable times of your life. We want to make sure you select a school that meets *all* of your needs.

Choosing which school to attend is a big decision. College is where you develop many of your lifelong friends; it can determine where you eventually live, what livelihood you choose after athletics, and the possibility of making a professional team. It's even where you may meet your future husband or wife.

So devote whatever time and energy you need from now until the end of your senior year to make sure you promote yourself in an intelligent and informative way. Although your parents, coaches, and teachers can help, your future rests in your hands. Are you motivated and determined enough to do the required work? We hope so, because the results of your efforts could pay dividends for the rest of your life.

Start Early

Don't wait until your senior year to begin your college search. As you will learn in this guide, finding the right school for you requires a continual effort over an extended period. We recommend you begin your search once you enter high school. If you are currently a junior or senior, your effort needs to be more intense and focused.

Maintain a Positive Attitude

Unfortunately, the college recruiting and search process can be filled with disappointments: You don't perform well in a big game, meet, or showcase event, you learn that your top school doesn't need an athlete like you, you don't have the statistics you hoped for, or no school offers you a scholarship. Whatever roadblocks you face, do your best not to get discouraged. Try to maintain a positive and upbeat attitude and have confidence that you will ultimately reach your goal. Confidence is an important key to success in life, not just on the athletic field.

Assumptions

If you are reading this guide, we assume that your knowledge about the college recruiting process is limited. You probably feel confused and are unsure what steps you should take to attract the attention of college recruiters. Most of your anxiety can be avoided if you understand the recruiting process. That's where we can help.

> **Catch This**
>
> Think of the process as a job search. If you were looking for employment, would you wait for companies to call you? Of course not! You'd be proactive and let companies know that you want to be hired. That's what you need to do here.

This guide is loaded with useful information to give you the confidence and skills you need to market yourself and to identify and attend the school of your dreams.

We're also assuming that few coaches outside of your local area know your name, even if you're an outstanding athlete with tons of potential. Furthermore, athletes from warm weather climates who compete in outdoor sports have the advantage of training year-round, generally making them more skilled and experienced athletes than those from cold weather climates.

The opposite is true for a sport such as ice hockey, where a cold climate is definitely advantageous! Although you may be at a disadvantage because of where you live, don't be discouraged. We're going to show you how to generate attention from coaches all around the country, whether you live in sunny San Diego, California, or chilly Bangor, Maine.

Get Your Degree

There are countless stories of high school athletes who seek lucrative professional contracts but never get them. We want you to realize that you have a much better chance of becoming a successful businessperson, doctor, or lawyer if you graduate from college first. Once you receive a college degree, no one can ever take it away from you. It can help lead the way to financial security for the rest of your life.

Let Others Help You

It is important that you share this guide and advice with your parents, coaches, guidance counselors, and anyone else assisting you with your college search. You will benefit immensely from the opinions and experiences of people who have your best interests at heart and have been down this road before.

New Information

We've improved this to include several new features, including a section on how to best present yourself during showcase camps and other events where college coaches scout potential recruits. This information alone will give you a decided edge over other athletes attending these events.

Why We Wrote This Guide

Since 1991, our company has worked with thousands of young athletes with dreams of competing on the collegiate level. Even though most of these top athletes aspired to compete at the college level, few of them got the chance and their careers ended prematurely. We couldn't understand why this was happening, so we decided to learn everything we could about the college recruiting process and share it all with you.

The information we've compiled during the last fourteen years features extensive research with hundreds of college coaches, guidance counselors, high school players, and parents.

Catch This
This guide is written for high school athletes who want to compete at the collegiate level and receive a college degree. It is not written for blue-chip athletes who receive national publicity, genuine interest from top schools, and invitations to the country's top tournaments or events.

Here's What We've Concluded:

The reasons that so many talented student-athletes never realize their dreams of competing in college include the following:

- They don't understand the recruiting process.
- They don't apply to appropriate schools.
- They don't prepare academically and athletically.
- They don't promote themselves properly.

We don't want this to happen to you!

With thousands of college athletic programs in the United States, we know there is a school out there that needs an athlete just like you. Now, let's go find it!

Master the Recruiting Process

In this chapter:

- ☐ How college coaches recruit
- ☐ Where they go to find their athletes
- ☐ A college coach's A-list
- ☐ When the peak recruiting season is
- ☐ The kinds of background checks coaches do

- ☐ How a coach expresses interest in a recruit
- ☐ Some basic facts about scholarships
- ☐ Pitfalls to avoid in the recruiting process

This chapter covers the basic—and not-so-basic—information about the recruiting process. By the end of this chapter, you should have a better understanding of how it all works.

How a College Coach Thinks about Recruiting

You will have an enormous advantage over your competition if you are familiar with the recruiting process from a college coach's standpoint. Not every college recruits exactly as described here—coaches at smaller schools have less money to recruit and may travel less than their Division I counterparts, for example—but the information presented here is typical of most athletic programs.

A Coach Is Always Looking for Top Athletes

A coach constantly keeps his ears and eyes open for athletes who can help his team. Naturally, he spends the majority of his time focusing on his next recruiting class. However, if you are a talented underclassman and you impressed a college coach—either at a camp, a game, or a meet or from a newspaper article he read about you—he will probably keep your name in his recruiting database and follow your development.

Chalk Talk

"I want team-oriented players with the ability to make decisions quickly on the field. I look for speed, quickness, and toughness. I use a lot of video in my decisions, and I certainly like to see each player in person when possible."

—Ben DeLuca, Cornell University, Assistant Lacrosse Coach, NCAA D-I

Coaches Help One Another Recruit

College coaches belong to a very small fraternity. Many are good friends, work the same summer camps, and socialize at annual conventions. Also, many coaches change jobs frequently and devote a lot of time to maintaining their professional network of contacts. On occasion, they even share information about top athletes and assist one another with recruiting (assuming they are not rivals in the same conference).

Few college coaches can recruit every outstanding athlete he or his staff sees. If a desirable athlete's grades don't meet his school's requirements or if the athlete plays a specific position and the coach is already stocked at that position, the coach may recommend the athlete to other coaches he knows.

That's why it's important to develop relationships with as many coaches as you can. If a college camp coach is really impressed with you, make an effort to stay in touch with him via mail or e-mail. Update him on your development. Even if he doesn't coach at a school that interests you, he could be your ticket to a college scholarship somewhere else. Remember, it's not who you know but who knows you!

Developing an A-List

When the recruiting process begins each year, coaching staffs assemble an A-list of high school juniors they are interested in recruiting. The names on this list are athletes that the coaches have seen in action at a camp, state and national meets, or tournaments. The names also come from referrals by trusted sources, such as other college coaches, boosters, former athletes, sports reporters, pro scouts, credible recruiting services, and some high school coaches. Many junior college coaches also keep an eye out for late-developing seniors.

It is important to remember that coaches' A-lists are composed of high school juniors-to-be, meaning that they appeared on the coaches' radar long before the students' junior years. With this in mind, place yourself in position to be noticed or evaluated by recruiters before your junior year.

This can be accomplished by playing for prominent summer league teams, participating in college camps held by the schools you are interested in, attending showcase camps that college coaches attend, and personally notifying the coach of your interest in his program and letting him know your qualifications.

Determining Who Is Interested

Questionnaires are sent to every athlete on a coach's A-list as well as to any athlete who writes or phones the coach's office expressing interest in the program. If you receive a questionnaire, you will be asked to provide detailed academic and athletic information about yourself and to return the form promptly. If you neglect to

return it quickly, be aware that you are sending a strong message that you are not interested in being recruited. Some elite athletes on the A-list who do not return their questionnaires may receive a follow-up phone call to determine their interest level, but most will not.

Working with Admissions Officers to Narrow Down the List

Coaches meet periodically with their college's admissions officer liaison to discuss prospective recruits. This is where your ability on the playing field can help you get admitted to a good academic school that you might not qualify for on

Hold Up

Returning the questionnaire promptly does more than tell the coach you are interested in his program. It also tells him or her that you are conscientious, able to follow instructions, and attentive to detail. Sometimes, little things like that can make all the difference in the world. While you may not stand out from the crowd by doing this, you'll definitely stand out if your questionnaire comes in late, is sloppy, or lacks important information.

grades or test scores alone. A coach will compile a list of his top recruits so that the liaison knows which athletes are the coach's highest priorities.

Making evaluations based on academic credentials, the liaison will often tell the coach who has a chance to be admitted and who does not. Some admissions departments are flexible and accept top recruits who may fall slightly below the academic requirements, but this happens only if you are in high demand by the coaching staff.

The coaching staff will then begin to reduce its A-list to a more manageable and realistic pool of candidates. It will only contain students who can contribute athletically, fill a position need on the team, and possess the academic marks to get accepted to the school.

In-Home Visits

Some coaches visit top recruits in their homes. If a head coach or assistant coach comes to your house, he will want to meet with you, your parents, and maybe your high school coach. The coach's goal is to explain the benefits of his school's academic program and team, discuss scholarships and financial aid, and determine your interest level in his school. Obviously, he also wants to get to know you as a person and make sure he is making a wise investment of his time, coaching resources, and, possibly, scholarship funds.

NCAA Clearinghouse

An NCAA member coach will require confirmation from the NCAA Clearinghouse that you are academically eligible to compete in college sports. If you have not achieved the required grades, test scores, and courses, the coach will immediately eliminate you from his recruiting list. Don't get knocked out of the recruiting game before it even starts by underachieving in class. See chapter 7 for more information on the NCAA Clearinghouse.

Core Courses

The NCAA requires a certain number of college preparatory (core) courses to be completed in high school before an athlete is eligible to play his or her freshman year. This requirement recently changed from thirteen to fourteen, and it's possible that it may change again.

Make sure in your freshman year that you know the current requirement for your graduating class and that you are taking enough core courses to qualify. If athletes have insufficient core courses when they graduate, they will not be allowed to participate in their sport during their freshman year of college and they will not be allowed to receive an athletic scholarship.

Athletes who fail to complete the required number of core courses will be allowed to play their sophomore year and receive scholarships, but the sad truth is that their year of inactivity may cost them a valuable scholarship as the coach may opt for another player.

Therefore, it is imperative that you make sure at the start of your freshman year that you have planned your academic schedule to include enough core courses and that you do so each year until you graduate. It's also best to try to complete core courses as early as you can in your high school career in the event that you fail one of these required courses. You'll want to have enough time left in your high school career to make it up!

Coaches Do Their Homework, Too

Before a coach decides to offer you a scholarship, he will do an extensive background check to find out everything he can about you. A scholarship is a big financial risk for the coach and his/her college, so coaches can be very thorough in their research, in order to improve the chances of making an intelligent decision. A few phone calls to your high school coach, guidance counselor, teachers, summer team coach, friends, and any local contacts he has will provide the information he needs.

So Ask Yourself Right Now:

■ Is there anything I am doing now that will negatively affect a college coach's opinion of me?

■ Do I attend all of my classes?

- Do I get along with my teammates?
- Am I a leader or a follower?
- What kind of crowd do I hang out with?
- How is my work ethic, drive, and integrity?

Scholarships and Walk-Ons

Once the athletic staff has finalized its recruiting list, it's time to decide which incoming freshmen or transfer students will receive athletic scholarships and how much money each person will receive. All other athletes on the recruiting list will be invited to try to make the team as walk-ons, assuming they still want to attend the school.

Telephone Calls

College coaches are not allowed to call you until the July 1 before the start of your senior year. You are permitted to call a college coach as often as you like, but do not abuse this privilege and acquire the dreaded "nuisance" tag. After July 1, a coach is limited to one outgoing phone call to you per week, except during these situations:

- Five days before your official campus visit
- On the day of a coach's off-campus visit with you
- On the initial date for signing the national letter of intent and two days after that

Letter of Intent

At the NCAA D-I level, there is an early signing period and a late signing period where a coach will try to persuade his top recruits who have been offered athletic scholarships to sign a national letter of intent. This letter is a binding contract that guarantees that the recruit will enroll at a specific school.

Facts about Scholarships

The number of full scholarships that each school can distribute is strictly limited. Each coach decides how to award his scholarship allotment. It makes the most sense to divide the allotment into several partial scholarships as opposed to giving only a few athletes full scholarships. It's a lower-risk strategy because some of the scholarship recipients will fall short of expectations, get injured, become academically ineligible, or drop out.

Also, realize that the scholarships are not just earmarked for incoming freshmen but are used for all athletes on the team. This may include as many as thirty-five sophomores, juniors, seniors, and fifth-year athletes. The number of scholarships also varies by sport—baseball and softball, for instance, have 11.7 and 12.0 total scholarships. Other sports, such as football, will have even more on a squad (also more scholarships but not enough for the entire team), while a sport such as basketball or fencing will have fewer, naturally.

The point is that there are very few sports in which a coach can offer every participant a full ride. What also may happen is that an upperclassman may have his or her scholarship amount increased in an effort to retain that player. A quarter scholarship may be improved to a half scholarship, for instance. Which means the "extra" scholarship money has to come from another athlete.

As a result, thousands of outstanding high school athletes are never offered even partial scholarships. Many don't even receive passing interest from coaches. Keep in mind that schol-

> **Catch This**
>
> NCAA D-I and D-II schools must wait until September 1 of your junior year before sending you promotional items, such as school or team publications, media guides, and playing schedules.

arships are awarded on a year-to-year basis. While a coach cannot guarantee that you will receive the same award in future years, it is normal practice that it will be renewed at the same level.

Even if you are fortunate enough to get all or some of your tuition paid for with an athletic scholarship, you may still have other significant costs, such as room and board, books, entertainment, and transportation to and from school. D-III and D-I Ivy League and Patriot League schools do not offer any athletic scholarships (American University, a Patriot League member, is the exception). Military academies such as Air Force, West Point, Navy, and Coast Guard are tuition-free; however, admission requires a congressional recommendation.

In addition to allocating scholarships, a coach can consult with financial aid officers on your behalf to determine what nonathletic aid might be available. However, you should personally check out for yourself other areas of help since you cannot expect the coach to explore all available options for each prospect.

Real Stories: One Runner's Lost Opportunity

Samantha Kent, twenty-one years old, Brooklyn, New York

In high school, training occupied most of my time. Unfortunately, I spent my time away from the track in college. My friends back home couldn't understand how an All-County sprinter could just give it up. Truth is, I didn't give it up; I just never gave myself a chance to run.

I was convinced a college coach would offer me a track scholarship. Instead of following the aggressive approach one of my friends took, I waited for college coaches to come to me. I was sure I would be noticed.

My times were good enough to get some attention, so there was no need to worry. No one told me I had to take the initiative and write letters and attend national meets. What a mistake! Now I'm a college senior, on the verge of graduating, and I never stepped foot on the track. I couldn't even bring myself to attend any meets; it was too frustrating.

I had a great time at school, but when I graduate in May, there will be an empty feeling inside of me. I should have competed. Running in college would have made everything complete. I know I could have competed. I was even friends with some of the others on the team.

It would have been a perfect fit. If I had only aggressively promoted myself in high school, I'm sure I would have had more options and a much more rewarding college experience.

Likely Letters

If you are offered an athletic scholarship, you must inform the college in November or April if you are going to accept it. Since you will not hear from the admissions or financial aid office until mid-April that you have been accepted to the school and offered a financial aid package, you will receive a "likely letter."

This states whether you are likely or unlikely to be accepted to the school and receive a financial aid package. The likely letter allows you to make an informed decision about where to go to school without forcing you to *void the scholarship*.

Twelve Pitfalls to Avoid

Most high school athletes never get the opportunity to compete in college. It's important for you to understand the main reasons why this happens. Avoid their mistakes and you will substantially improve your chances of competing in college.

1. I Only Want to Compete for a High-Profile NCAA D-I Team.

If you only focus your search on the country's top programs, you will be disappointed. Too many high school athletes think that programs such as UCLA, Florida State, Miami, Stanford, Michigan, and other high-profile schools are the only respectable ones in the country.

While many high school athletes dream of one day competing at a top NCAA Division I school, in reality, very few get the opportunity. According to our research, roughly 2 percent of all high school and junior college athletes who seek to compete at a D-I school will ever get the chance.

If you're just finishing your junior year of high school, you'll have a pretty good idea if you are talented enough to compete at that level. Blue-chip athletes recruited by these nationally ranked schools

- Are often All-State or All-County award recipients
- Receive recruiting calls and letters from numerous coaches
- Attract many college coaches to their games

LESSON LEARNED If you are not a blue-chip recruit, expand your college search to include a range of schools on your Target List.

> **Chalk Talk**
>
> "I'd say 75 percent of athletes don't research schools like they should. I tell them to look at it like a twenty-one-year-old adult, rather than a seventeen-year-old kid. In four years, I want them to look back and see that they made the right decision. They have to pick the best fit for them, not the biggest name. College is expensive; you want to make sure you do the right thing."
>
> —*Amy Hayes, Boston University, Head Softball Coach, NCAA D-I*

2. I Must Be a Hot Recruit. Coaches Send Me Letters All the Time.

Do not assume form letters in your mailbox mean that a coach considers you a prospect. Every high school athlete who expresses interest in a college team, regardless of his ability, will receive a letter and questionnaire in the mail asking for more information. In fact, some D-I schools may send out as many as ten thousand letters each year! Understand that this is only an initial request for information and, in most cases, an expected courtesy. Answer the following questions honestly:

- Do college coaches call me?
- Is my mailbox overflowing with letters from coaches who want me to consider their schools?

- Are coaches coming to my house to meet with my parents and me?
- Am I receiving all-expenses-paid invitations to campuses?
- Do recruiters travel specifically to watch me compete?

If you're one of the lucky few who can answer yes to some of these questions, then consider yourself a blue-chip prospect. If you're like most high school athletes, however, and you had to answer no to all or most of the questions, then you need to take a proactive approach to your college search.

LESSON LEARNED Receiving phone calls, personalized handwritten letters from college coaches, and requests for personal meetings is a much better indicator—rather than form letters and questionnaires—of how interested a coach is in recruiting you.

3. I'll Make the College Team as a Walk-On.

If you only receive lukewarm interest from coaches but you really want to compete in college, you can try making the team as a walk-on. This means that you try to prove yourself to the coaching staff in the fall or preseason tryouts. Your odds of success: not good.

However, understand that it may be difficult to make the team as a nonrecruited athlete. Every now and then, a coach may find a diamond in the rough who has gone unnoticed. For the most part, however, a coach knows exactly which athletes will form his squad before the open tryout even begins. This is another reason why it is a bad mistake to fail to match your actual skill level with the competitive skill level of the school at which you are trying to compete.

Chalk Talk

"We only have a few walk-ons each year. I urge those looking to walk on to contact coaches and let them know you are interested in the program. Then, just work on your skills and stay in shape."

—*Amy Barlett, Bryant College, Assistant Field Hockey Coach, NCAA D-II*

LESSON LEARNED Even if you make the team, you may have only a slim chance of ever competing. You may want to search harder for a school that wants you and that you fit with talentwise. Many athletes who try to walk on, not including "recruited walk-ons" (whom we discuss in chapter 5), may quit the team and transfer or drop out after their freshman year. Check out our "Hit the Web" section in chapter 4 for the best way to search for schools that fit your talent level.

4. My High School Coach Is Going to Get Me a Scholarship.

Do not rely on your high school coach to contact college coaches, write letters, or solicit offers on your behalf. Most high school coaches are unable or unwilling to devote the large amounts of time required to help their athletes find the right colleges. If your coach has time to assist you with the recruiting process and has demonstrated a commitment to help you find a school that meets your needs, consider yourself lucky.

Too frequently, we hear from parents that their child's high school coach doesn't do anything to help. Often these complaints come in the spring of a high school athlete's senior year, after most college application deadlines have already passed.

Don't worry if your coach only limits his involvement to practices and games. Some coaches, for whatever reason, do not believe that college recruiting is part of their job responsibility. Some are simply too busy to help. Others are unfamiliar with the recruiting process and might not even know where to begin.

Many coaches who sincerely want to help are restricted in their efforts simply because they don't have that many college contacts, except perhaps those who are local or are from the college the coaches themselves attended. While thankfully rare, there occasionally exists a coach who is vindictive for one reason or another simply because of a personality conflict!

While this is indeed rare, cases like this have happened. Just another reason why high school athletes need to take the initiative and take charge of their own recruiting processes. Some coaches devote all of their time to the star athlete because he's the easiest one to promote. Remember: What's on the line in the recruiting game is your future, not that of your coaches. Don't sit back and wait for someone to help you.

LESSON LEARNED Don't expect your high school coach to devote much time and effort to personally assist you with your college search. Ask him to help, but take responsibility and control your own future

5. I'd Be Happy Just to Make the Team.

Always set high goals for yourself. We have found that the athletes who have the best college experience are the ones who get the chance to compete on a regular basis. Staying at home while the team travels to an away game is no fun unless you have the potential to work your way into a more competitive role within a short period. You have to ask yourself, "Would I rather be the big fish in a small pond or a small fish in a big pond?"

LESSON LEARNED Find a team where you can contribute and have a realistic chance to compete.

6. Lots of College Coaches Will Watch My High School Games.

If more than a handful of college coaches ever watch you compete throughout your high school career, you are in a select group. Even if coaches attend your games, they most likely represent nearby schools.

Most athletic recruiting budgets do not allow coaches to travel around the country scouting talent. It's just too expensive. Coaches will scout regional high school and summer tournaments or events, usually within a couple of hours of their schools, but rarely will they travel farther. It's just not financially feasible or an efficient use of their time.

It's not unusual for a college coach to spend the majority of his travel and recruiting budget scouting a select few blue-chip prospects. What's left in the travel budget will be used to attend national events, where the greatest number of prospects can be seen in one place—that is, showcase events and regional or national tournaments.

Say, for example, you live in Minnesota and are interested in attending a college in Texas. Even if the coach in Texas really likes you, he probably won't have the money or the time to fly to Minnesota to watch you compete. He would rather find out if you are going to attend any events where he can see you and a number of other athletes on his list. Or he may invite you to attend one of his summer camps.

LESSON LEARNED Be proactive and take your skills to coaches of the schools that interest you. Don't expect them to travel to your hometown.

7. Small Colleges Have Weak Teams.

Most athletes believe the misconception that NCAA D-I is the only way to go and that all other college divisions are inferior. Don't fall into this trap! If you do, you will eliminate hundreds of great schools that may need an athlete just like you.

LESSON LEARNED Surprisingly, many D-II, D-III, NAIA, and junior college teams stack up well against D-I schools. Don't neglect them simply because of their affiliations.

8. I'm Only Considering Schools Where I Can Earn a Full Ride.

Full-ride scholarships are not as readily available as most athletes and parents think. Most scholarship money is divided into partial scholarships.

LESSON LEARNED Don't expect that an athletic scholarship will allow you to attend school for free. Even if you are one of the fortunate few to receive an athletic scholarship, you will probably still have to pay for other college expenses with family money, an academic scholarship, or loans.

Catch This
There's another reason that college coaches don't rely too heavily on a player's high school stats. They realize that high school officials and scorekeepers can inflate an athlete's statistics.

9. I'm Only Applying to My First-Choice School.

"It's the only place I want to attend." Even if your heart is set on attending one particular school and the coach has expressed interest in you, you should still promote yourself to other schools. It will give you leverage when it comes time to discuss academic and athletic scholarships or financial assistance with the coach and admissions office.

The coach at your first choice school has all the bargaining power if he finds out that you are desperate to attend his school. Plus, you might find that a different school—one you might not have thought of before—is a better fit for you.

LESSON LEARNED Leverage is crucial if you want to increase your worth and attain a better scholarship. Avoid the temptation to prematurely tell a coach that you've made your decision to attend his school.

10. I'm Regularly Told by High School or Summer League Coaches That I Have the Ability to Compete at the Division I Level.

Constant praise from influential people is nice to hear, but it can also be dangerous. It may cause you to sit back, to wait for college coaches to come to you, and to not be aggressive in your search.

LESSON LEARNED Always strive to improve your skills. Never stop learning. And, as they say in the business world, don't believe your own PR!

11. If A Coach from a School outside My Target List Wants to Recruit Me, I'll Tell Him I'm Not Interested.

Avoid rushing to judgment if a coach expresses interest in recruiting you. A lot can change in a few months. A school that you dismiss now may look a lot more attractive later on. Never lie to or mislead a coach, but you should also avoid making snap judgments. Make sure you research every opportunity before making up your mind.

> ### Chalk Talk
>
> "A lot of high school athletes have unrealistic expectations of themselves. This often prevents athletes from getting into the schools of their choice. Either they don't know the level of their own athletic ability, or their academics don't match their athletic ability."
>
> —*Cregg Weinmann, California State University, Bakersfield, Head Track Coach, NCAA D-II*

Once you decide exactly where you want to go and after you have signed a letter of intent, tell the other coaches who are interested in you to remove you from their recruiting lists. Make sure to thank them sincerely for their interest in you. Not only does it show good character, but if you ever want to transfer, that school can still be a good option.

LESSON LEARNED Keep your options open! Avoid rushing to judgment until you have made up your mind. You should also visit each school that shows interest in you—it's the best way to decide if it's a place that you not only want to compete for but make your new home as well.

12. Coaches Will Notice Me When I Have a Big Senior Season.

If you play a winter or spring sport, you may already know where you are going to college by the time your senior season is underway. Also, some coaches have already made up their A-list of recruits and narrowed it down to their top priority prospects by the fall of your senior year.

LESSON LEARNED Your junior year could be your most important recruiting period.

Energize Your Support Group

You are definitely not alone in the process of solving the college recruiting puzzle. There are many people ready and willing to help you if you just ask. You need to develop your own cast of advocates, first, to help you create a list of colleges best suited to you and, then, to help you apply and gain admission.

This chapter helps you identify and energize the people who can improve your chances of reaching your college athletic and academic goals. It includes some information specifically designed for your parents or guardians, the people who have the most at stake financially and emotionally in how your college selection process moves forward. So, even if they can't take the time to read this entire book, at least make sure they review this chapter with you.

For grammatical purposes, portions of this chapter are written to the male gender. All information is applicable to female athletes as well.

Parents

Dear Parent:

It's a challenge to strike the right balance between offering guidance to your child and taking control of the entire college search process. If he is like most teenagers, you will need to constantly provide gentle reminders so that he stays focused on the search.

In this chapter we discuss some of the ways to help him prepare for one of the biggest decisions and transitions of his young life. The objective: to help him get accepted to a college where he will receive the best education possible and have the opportunity to compete in collegiate sports—in that order.

It's a Big Country, so Think National

The United States is blessed with many wonderful things, including the best, largest, and most diverse higher-education system in the world. There are dozens of colleges that would be a good academic and athletic match for any high school athlete, including your son.

The first commandment of developing a Target List of appropriate schools is to start with an open mind and a blank slate. "What's the right school for my son?" is a multiple-choice question with more than one right answer.

Discourage him from fixating on a single "dream" school, unless he's an absolute lock to get in and is one of those unusual kids who knows exactly what he wants in life. Even then, we recommend you look at other institutions just in case he starts second-guessing himself later on.

It's Okay to Be Nervous, but Try Not to Grab the Wheel

Helping with the research and applying to colleges reminds you of the separation soon to come and the undeniable fact that your teenager is moving toward adulthood. This can make you nervous and emotional. You may feel tempted to take control of the evaluation and application process, particularly if he is not being as diligent and focused as you would like.

One simple word of advice: Don't! Your job is to support him in his efforts to make his own decision about college and his future. Managing this process on his own is a critical element in his mental and psychological preparation for leaving home. He can handle it, and so can you!

As the process unfolds, remind him that because he applied to a variety of colleges and also worked hard at his academics and athletics, he will be accepted to at least one of the schools on his Target List— one where he will make friends, have fun, be challenged, and get the education he deserves. When the decision letters arrive, reemphasize your support, and if necessary, remind him of the fickle nature of the whole selection process.

Stay in the Background

Nothing is worse than a parent who steals the spotlight. Many parents, especially successful ones, are accustomed to manipulating the system to make it work for them. Resist the temptation. The admission process is the time for your child to stand on his own. Parental attempts at influence peddling often do more harm than good.

> **Hold Up**
>
> If your plan for paying for your son's or daughter's education is basically "he/she will get a full-ride scholarship," you're probably in for a rude awakening. College athletic scholarships are hard to come by, and most do not cover all of your child's expenses. It's great to win the lottery but not too smart to plan on it happening.

Don't Live Vicariously

Many parents subconsciously relive their own hopes and dreams through their children. Some want their kids to follow in their footsteps; others want them to achieve things that they themselves never could. Still other parents see their children's college admission as proof they deserve an A-plus in parenting. Having high hopes for your child is natural, but try to spare him the burden of unreasonable expectations. One of the greatest gifts you can give him is the freedom and the support to follow his own dreams, not yours.

Communicate

Encourage your son or daughter to think through the basic questions:

- Why do I want to go to college?
- What are my most important needs and goals?

- What size school would I feel most comfortable?
- Do I want to stay close to home, within driving distance, or at least an airplane ride away?

Communicating with a teenager is not always easy, but look for the moments that present themselves, and they will. Being available to talk when he has a question or wants to express an idea or feeling is extremely important. This is probably the first time he is dealing with a decision of this magnitude, so try to be patient and give him the time and space to find a way to communicate what his thoughts and fears are.

Set Financial Parameters

Although we have been stressing that the college selection process should be managed by your child, there is one part of this picture over which you have the responsibility and the obligation to assert your control: dollars and cents.

If you're in the market for a Chevrolet, it doesn't make sense to spend a lot of time at the Mercedes dealer ogling cars you can't afford. Likewise, if your resources can't support a tuition of $30,000 per year, have that conversation with your son before starting to develop a Target List of schools. This will be a necessary and healthy dose of real life for both of you.

You and your child will be terribly disappointed if you end up falling in love with a school and a program that is simply beyond your means and you have to say, "Sorry, keep looking." Go online and find a list of all U.S. colleges sorted by tuition expense. Chapter 8 features a list of great websites to help you with your research. No matter what your budget, your son is sure to find plenty of schools to choose from.

Be Realistic

Don't set him up for failure by encouraging him to apply only to schools that may be out of reach. Look honestly at his academic record and athletic ability, and then study the admission profiles of the colleges on the Target List. If he is not Stanford material, don't swing by Palo Alto, California, on your college tour. Make sure he applies to at least two colleges where he is overqualified and can expect to be accepted. Then, even in the worst-case scenario, if he isn't accepted to his first-choice schools, he still has a viable plan B.

Encourage Your Child to Stay on Schedule

Review the high school checklist (see chapter 8) with your child to make sure he is staying on track and doing the required work. Don't let him procrastinate and put it off until his senior year of high school. Athletes who do their research and prepare early have the most opportunities.

Support, Support, Support!

You can lighten the workload by providing guidebooks and web addresses, returning questionnaires, assisting with background research, and following the advice in this guide. Just make sure to stay in the background, in a supportive role. If you discover a potential gem of a school, pass along the web address and let him explore it for himself.

Catch This
Your perception of your child's athletic ability will not earn a scholarship. The college coach's opinion and other respected and objective appraisals are the only ones that matter.

Share your own college decision-making memories. Convey your understanding of how intimidating the process can seem, and let him benefit from your experience.

Be a Cheerleader

Be generous with your praise for his accomplishments. Remind him that the acceptance or rejection to a particular school will not change his worth as an individual. The world is filled with highly accomplished people who didn't attend prestigious universities.

Encourage Your Child to Focus on Academics

The higher his grades and test scores, the more sports opportunities he will have. Make academics a priority and do whatever is necessary to convey the importance of raising his marks. If he is not reaching his academic potential, find someone who can help him, whether it's a private tutor, a teacher, or one of his friends. Make sure that you make this assessment early on in his academic career so that both of you will have time to increase his potential.

Senior year is too late to address this issue! Be aware that there are some student-athletes who figure that their senior year is a time to take it easy and enjoy their last year of high school. This is the time that some students' grades take a nosedive. Don't let this "senioritis" happen to your son! College admissions people frown on this and are aware of this phenomenon. It's not uncommon for an offer to be withdrawn in the event of a shoddy senior academic year.

"Academic" Athletic Showcases

Some specialized showcases are now inviting only talented athletes with superior grades and/or SAT or ACT scores. These showcases are held for Ivy League universities and other institutions that don't offer athletic scholarships. Schools such as Rice, Notre Dame, Stanford, and Northwestern University fit this category. Even though the Ivy League and Patriot League don't provide athletic scholarships, they often assist the athlete with academic scholarships and grants. Besides athletic ability, players invited to these specialized showcases may have to meet at least one of the following academic criteria: 3.3 grade point average, 1100 SAT score, or 24 ACT score.

Discuss Majors and Potential Careers

Talk about potential majors that may interest your son. Ask him what he would like to do for his career. He may not have an answer, but it's something he should be thinking about. Encourage him to seek advice from successful family friends who work in his areas of interest. In many parts of the country, there are opportunities for high school students to "shadow" someone in the field they're interested in—that is, spend a day on the job with that person.

Also, there are mentoring opportunities for students to be advised and guided by someone in the field they're interested in. Coaches are impressed by students who have clear career goals or who at least have put some thought into what they want to do after sports. It's a sign of maturity many coaches appreciate and value.

Visit College Campuses

From the time your child enters high school, make an effort to visit as many different college campuses as you can. You can attend sporting events, concerts, or campus tours. Let him experience the colleges that you or other family members attended.

If your family takes vacations, visit schools in that area. Once he reaches junior year of high school, limit your visits to schools that he is seriously considering. Schedule your trips so that there is time to watch the teams work out or compete. These unofficial visits will give enormous insight and help decide what kind of school he wants to attend.

> ### Chalk Talk
>
> "If you don't get it done in the classroom, you can become ineligible or distract yourself from the job on the field. I look for players to be sharp, look sharp, play hard, and maintain those grades. If I don't have to worry about them in class, then we can concentrate on softball."
>
> —*Scot Thomas, Head Softball Coach, Virginia Tech University, NCAA D-I*

Get Periodic Updates

It is important to periodically phone or meet with your son's teachers, guidance counselor, and coach. This will keep you informed of his progress and allow you to confirm that he is staying on course and meeting academic requirements.

Don't Write Your Child's Application Essay

Many colleges require essays as part of their application processes. Advisors caution parents not to edit their son's or daughter's essays, since admissions officers can distinguish easily between the writing of a forty-five-year-old and that of a seventeen-year-old. Instead, review the application folder for mistakes or omissions. Once it has been sent, do not call, write, or e-mail the admissions office. All communication should come from your child.

Step Aside

If your child gets rejected at a particular school, the worst thing you can do is call the school and tell them they overlooked something. Admissions officers are more apt to listen to a direct appeal from your child than from a disappointed parent.

Also, resist the temptation to call coaches and write letters on his behalf. Most college coaches would rather communicate with an athlete than a parent. It demonstrates that he is mature and responsible.

Split Up on College Visits

Many counselors advise parents to avoid the temptation of accompanying their children everywhere on campus. You may even want to skip the guided campus tour and let him experience it by himself. Most admissions officers won't allow parents into the interview but will entertain a few questions afterward. While you wander around campus, he can sit in on classes, talk to professors, and hang out with students.

Deal with Rejection

If the dreaded rejection letter arrives from his top-choice school, don't turn his disappointment into your own. With this response, he is apt to feel as though he has failed you, too. Let him mourn his dream. Be around in case he wants to talk about it. Tell him that from your perspective, it doesn't matter where he goes to college. Say that you are sorry and that you know he's disappointed. Leave it at that. Focus on the schools that accept him.

Guidance Counselor

For better or worse, your guidance counselor is likely to play a crucial part in your college search and application process. He will write recommendations for you that, come April of your senior year, will help determine whether you receive fat envelopes full of enrollment materials or skinny ones with rejection letters.

He will monitor phone calls from admissions officers with questions about a low grade on your transcript or a discipline problem. And if you wind up getting rejected everywhere you applied, a sympathetic counselor might even plead your case to admissions officials at schools that still have open slots. These are professionals you definitely want in your corner, so don't be shy about making the first move. It's also advantageous to include someone whose primary perspective is academic.

Real Stories: One Parent's Mistake

Alyssa Williams, New Haven, CT

In high school, my son Aaron was a three-year starter on the varsity team and was voted team MVP his senior season. He wasn't the most dominant player in our region, but everyone knew who he was. I figured he would have college coaches offering scholarships to him. I couldn't have been more wrong! By the start of his junior season, I was expecting coaches to show up at his games to watch him play. Aaron expressed interest in a couple of college programs by sending introductory letters during the previous winter. He even got some responses back with questionnaires attached. After I met with his high school coach, I was confident the coach would use his connections to help get Aaron a baseball scholarship. His coach knew a lot of people at the collegiate level and assured me everything would work out.

As his senior season approached, a lot of Aaron's friends were getting accepted to schools. I told him to go out and put up the kind of stats he was capable of and everything would fall into place. Aaron finished his senior year as a member of the All-County team with a .448 BA, 12 HR, 47 RBI, and 0 scholarship offers. They say mothers know best, but in this case, I didn't. I should have encouraged Aaron to take a more proactive approach promoting himself to college coaches. Luckily, his grades were good enough to get accepted to a strong academic college. He was even the star center fielder on his team . . . his fraternity's intramural squad.

Learn Your Way around the Office

While your guidance counselor is getting to know you, get to know your counselor's resources. Ask for a tour of the guidance office and have the counselor recommend college guidebooks, videotapes, and websites. Find out whether your high school hosts workshops on college admission. If it does, you should attend every session possible.

Use Your Counselor's Connections

Your best college resource may be your counselor's connections. If your counselor visits a lot of campuses and invites many admissions officers to your school, he's probably plugged into the college admission scene. Admissions officers who know and trust him may call for the inside scoop on you. And he will know which schools are most likely to accept you, which ones should be considered as "safeties," and which ones are long shots. We're stating the obvious here, but take advantage of this professional's knowledge!

Provide Good (and Bad) Information

If your counselor is too swamped for frequent personal chats with you, drop off a resume that lists your recent accomplishments. Create a portfolio of your best papers and creative projects, and don't be shy about disclosing any family situations that may affect your academic performance. For instance, if one of your parents gets seriously ill and your grades slip as a result, tell your counselor so that he can explain the situation in his recommendation. Once you establish a personal rapport with your counselor, e-mail may be a more acceptable way to stay in touch on routine matters.

Regular Meetings

Your counselor should meet with you and your parents for a conference at least once in your junior year and again early in your senior year. Topics can include your academic strengths and weaknesses, sports, test scores, whether you should take a prep class, and suggestions for colleges to consider.

He can also confirm if you are in compliance with NCAA eligibility requirements, explore potential career opportunities, identify colleges that specialize in your area of interest, and discuss the pros and cons of each school on your Target List.

Although most counselors are conscientious and knowledgeable, occasionally they may make an honest mistake, which could cost you a scholarship. Here's a real-life example of a high school player who took Spanish I in junior high (eighth grade) and Spanish II and III as a freshman and sophomore in high school.

His guidance counselor said that colleges would consider those courses as three years of a language. As it turned out, that was true of the state university where he lived but wasn't for lots of out-of-state colleges who only counted it as two years. The young man failed to qualify at the school he wanted to play for, which happened to be an out-of-state school with different requirements.

Real Stories: Overcoming Failure

by Tom Hanson, Ph.D.

Redefine "failure." Your personal statistics and your team's record are outside of your control. You can influence them but not control them. Focus your energies on things you can control: your preparation, your focus, your attitude, your commitment. If you define success as doing a great job with the things you can control and failure as focusing on things you can't control, you'll give yourself the best chance of competing at a top level *and* be a lot happier!

Focus on this moment. There's nothing you can do about the past and nothing you can do now about the future. *Now* is where the action is! The great athletes keep it simple, and one way to do that is to keep your focus consistent. If you've had a bad day, go ahead and feel bad for a while; that's okay. But remember, your poor performance is in the *past*. Before you go to bed that night, shift your focus to what you can control *now*: getting yourself into the best possible mind-set for next week's game.

These ideas are simple but not easy. Partner up with a buddy, coach, or parent to help you stay focused.

Tom Hanson, Ph.D., is a mental-toughness coach who helps athletes, coaches, and parents produce breakthrough results. Last year he worked full-time for the New York Yankees, and he has consulted with the Texas Rangers, Anaheim Angels, and Minnesota Twins.

The point is, make sure you check out and know the academic requirements of the schools you'd like to play for and attend. A good place to start is to check the NCAA eligibility site, as well as the school's admissions office.

Grades are important! One coach said he receives about two hundred to three hundred e-mails a week from parents and players expressing interest in his program. When asked how he begins to weed the prospects and interested players out, he replied, "It's pretty easy. Grades!"

Help Developing a Plan and Timetable

Many counselors believe their job is not to tell students where to apply but to advise them how to go about the process. Doing the legwork for students, counselors say, won't teach them the survival skills they need for college. A good counselor will direct you toward books and online resources. We will direct you to chapter 4, where we tell you how to identify appropriate colleges for you and develop what we call your *Target List*.

Use History to Help You

Generally, high schools keep lists of where previous students have and haven't been accepted. Schools with more sophisticated programs maintain a database on the records of students who were accepted and rejected at various colleges. Counselors should analyze the data to athletic admission trends and use them to guide applicants. Organized feedback from high school graduates about what they like and dislike about their colleges and about how prepared they felt academically is also useful information for you.

Be Vigilant

If you are put on a waiting list at your first-choice college, your counselor can call the college to promote you and let the admissions department know you really want to go there. If the outlook is dim, your counselor can provide suggestions about alternatives. If a qualified student strikes out everywhere (a high schooler's worst nightmare), a dedicated counselor can call around to find out which colleges have space available.

Find a Counselor Who Will Help

While it may be tempting to avoid your counselor, that's almost always a mistake. If your counselor resists all advances or simply doesn't know enough about colleges to be helpful, make an appointment with another counselor at your school. If asked, tell your assigned counselor that you are doing it as a way to gather additional information.

You can also consider going outside the school for college advice. But be warned that your high school counselor can't be avoided entirely. He still writes your recommendation, and colleges will still call him, not the independent advisor, if a school wants to know more about you. Never fear, though. College admissions committees know that, for a variety of reasons, not everyone receives adequate counseling—or a fair recommendation.

Counselors for Hire

You could hire an educational consultant to help you develop a list of schools and prepare applications. Their services usually cost from $700 to several thousand dollars (ouch!). Princeton Review and Kaplan Test Prep and Admissions offer one-on-one counseling. Less-personalized counseling is available in seminars or online packages. If you are truly needy, you can turn to groups such as Bottom Line, which counsels students for free. Many pricey consultants also offer free counseling, so don't be afraid to ask.

Red Flags

No matter what type of independent counselor you choose to work with, be sure to first check out one's qualifications. Reputable counselors belong to either the Independent Educational Consultants Association (703-591-4850) or the National Association for College Admission Counseling (800-822-6285).

Ask prospective counselors for professional references, and call them. A few things to avoid: inexperienced consultants who claim their Ivy League degrees give them special insight into the admission process, independent counselors who have cantankerous relationships with guidance offices (you can't afford to alienate your high school counselor!), and consultants who promise entrance into prestigious schools before viewing your academic record. Sounds too good to be true because it is.

High School Coach

Take Responsibility for Your College Search.

Do not depend on your high school coach to research potential schools, phone coaches on your behalf, or eventually land you a college scholarship. If your high school coach is supportive and wants to help you, consider yourself fortunate and be sure to thank him.

Don't worry, however, if your high school coach is not as involved as you would like and only devotes time to team practices and games. Even though you would like to believe your coach is responsible for helping you with your college search, it is not officially part of his job responsibilities. Remember, you have many teammates who would like the same kind of personal interest from him. So, if your

---

Real Stories: A Guidance Counselor's Plea

Richard Douds, High School Guidance Counselor, Raleigh, NC

I get paid to give advice. I only wish more students would make me earn my money. A lot of students come to me for academic advice, but I'm equally qualified to help them advance athletically. My high school guidance counselor played lacrosse for Wake Forest University and knew what the recruiting process was all about. He helped me get a lacrosse scholarship using his connections, and I would love to do the same for my kids, no matter what sport they play. Unfortunately, they don't come to me for help.

Aside from office resources, I have a number of connections to Division III schools on the East Coast. Some of the coaches my kids have contacted call me for recommendations. It's tough for me to promote someone if they haven't taken the time to come see me first.

Once I get to know him on a personal level, it's easier to give college coaches the information they want. I would love to help students develop a plan to achieve their athletic goals. Many of my colleagues don't know a lot about the recruiting process and wouldn't know what to say to a student looking to play at the collegiate level.

I tell them to have their students come talk to me if they want advice. It's really no burden. I have no problem calling college coaches to promote one of our athletes, but he needs to make the effort to come see me first.

---

coach wants to help you, gratefully accept his assistance. If he doesn't make the offer or respond to your request, take full responsibility for your future.

Ask Your High School Coach to Initiate Dialogue with Your Target Coaches

After you mail your letter of interest and athlete profile to your Target List (see chapter 5), ask your high school coach if he would be willing to do some or all of the following:

- Write an evaluation of you and send it to your target schools
- Phone each coach on your Target List to confirm the school's interest in you and give a verbal recommendation

---

Real Stories: A High School Coach's Conflict

Coach Mike Rivera, Baltimore, Maryland

My students assume my day starts at 7:20 am. In reality, my day starts well before that. My thirty-minute commute north from Annapolis starts around 6:30 am, and I'm awake an hour before that. I teach math five out of eight periods and also hold advising and office hours. When I'm not in the classroom, I'm grading tests, tutoring students, and devising lesson plans. A lot of my students end their day with the last bell, around 1:45 pm. At this point, I've been out of my house for nearly eight hours, and my day is only beginning.

At the end of eighth period, I replace lesson plans with game plans. Aside from my duties in the classroom, I'm also the head coach of two different sports. I hold daily practices from 2:30–5:00 pm, and on game days, we're usually done around 8:00 pm. Fifteen-hour days are tough, especially with a half-hour commute tacked on to either side.

A lot of my players ask me to help them get scholarships, and I do the best I can to assist them, but there isn't enough time in the day. I try to write evaluations for all my players and call college coaches on their behalf, but I can't help everyone. I know how stressful the recruiting and college selection process can be on my runners and their parents, which puts me in an awkward situation.

I would love to help all of my players get scholarships, but it's more important for me to see my students pass math. First and foremost, I'm a teacher. When I was a kid, I used to eat, sleep, and breathe sports. Now, I'm lucky if I have time to simply eat and sleep.

- Clarify the college's decision-making process
- Stimulate interest if the coach is not recruiting you

Use Other Sources for Help

Find someone who will assist you if your high school coach cannot. This person must be someone who has credibility and is familiar with your skills:

- Opposing high school coach
- College coach

- Former athlete who gives you lessons
- Summer team coach
- Alumnus in your sport of one of your target schools

Finish Line

Part of the recruiting process is taking stock of your assets for a college's team and its admissions department. And part of getting recruited is taking stock of the assets you have to draw on during the process itself.

Sit down, separately, with your parents, coach, and counselor. Tell them about your goals and dreams for college. Ask them for help in the process, and come to an agreement about how much help they will provide and what type of help it will be. Then make a list of all your resources and determine how you will use them to help you get recruited.

How to Improve Your Profile

No matter how many compliments you've received about your achievements, your grades, or your personality, there are always ways you can improve.

This chapter focuses on ways to improve your profile (and no, we don't mean the side view of your face) so that you are more recruitable by college coaches.

Athletic Suggestions

At the risk of stating the obvious, your athletic ability is the most important factor in determining whether you will suit up in a college uniform. Never assume that you are finished learning as an athlete or that you know everything about your sport. You must constantly absorb information and strive to improve your ability.

Even professional athletes spend hundreds of hours in the off-season working on the physical and mental aspects of their game, so you know there's no such thing as too much practice for a high school or college athlete.

Understand What's in Your Control to Improve

Some physical characteristics, such as your height and body structure, may not change, but there are many things within your control that you can improve. These areas include

- Strength
- Flexibility
- Endurance
- Speed
- Mental toughness

You'll have to work extremely hard and demonstrate unyielding motivation in order to separate yourself from the thousands of other athletes who are looking to play at the college level. If you know you are weak in a particular aspect of your event, do something about it . . . now!

Seek Constructive Criticism

To improve, first identify which areas of your athletic performance need work. It's always nice to hear praise from your parents and receive backslaps from your teammates, but a little constructive criticism from the experts is even better. Instead of relying on your parents' opinion of your skills, consult an experienced high school coach, college coach, or professional athlete who has seen you compete. He or she can tell you the exact areas to improve and recommend specific drills to help you.

Seek as many opinions as you can. For example, ask your coach to be completely honest and forthcoming about your strengths and weaknesses. You may not agree with his evaluation, but you can use it as a starting point for your development. It is also important to respect his opinion and let him know that you are going to consider his advice. In addition to learning where your game could use some improving, make sure you set aside the time for drills to help turn your weaknesses into strengths.

If you have mechanical flaws, fix them immediately to avoid making them a permanent part of your technique. Videotaping yourself in a practice setting is an excellent way for you to recognize exactly what you are doing wrong, and it's a great way to solicit feedback from others who haven't seen you compete much or at all.

Take Your Game to the Coaches

Exposure is key to the recruiting process. The more coaches who see you perform, the better chance you have to generate interest. Don't wait for coaches to come to you. Be proactive and take your game to them.

Your goal should be to generate as much national interest as you can so that you will have an array of options when it comes time to sign a national letter of intent. If you live in New York and want to compete in North Carolina, you better make sure Southern coaches see you compete in person.

It is unusual for a coach to offer a scholarship to an athlete that no one on his staff has seen compete. It's too much of a risk. That's why you need to find out how you can compete in front of the coaches on your Target List.

Call each school and ask the coach what tournaments or showcases his recruiters are attending. Also, ask them to put you on their mailing lists to be notified of winter and summer camps (as well as any special camps) and any other pertinent information. Just make sure the coaches on your Target List see you in action.

How Many of These Leadership Qualities Do You Possess?

- Have a strong desire to win and always do my best
- Seek tough competition
- Welcome a difficult task
- Set high but achievable goals
- Be willing to admit mistakes and accept constructive criticism
- Practice on my own—go beyond what my coach asks of me
- Enjoy the responsibility that accompanies leadership
- Be willing to work harder than anyone else, especially when the coach is not watching
- Possess confidence in my ability

- Focus and concentrate on the task at hand
- Learn from my mistakes and try not to repeat them
- Maintain composure
- Don't get easily discouraged or frustrated by errors, mistakes, or poor officiating
- Understand the importance of continual coaching
- Respect coaches, officials, teammates, and opponents
- Put the team's needs before my personal needs
- Get along with my teammates—offer support when they have a problem
- Understand that championships are won in the preseason
- Watch my language and avoid profanity
- Encourage my teammates and do not belittle my opponents.
- Maintain positive appearance and body language
- Respect my parents and coaches

What Motivates a Winner . . .

Coach Rob Kelso, University of Houston

- A winner displays characteristics that set him apart from all others.
- A winner always wants to be the best that he can be.
- A winner is never satisfied with his performance. He is committed to preparing and is open to change, and he always wants to succeed, whether it's a high GPA or a better athletic performance.
- A winner learns from his failures and never makes excuses.
- A winner always looks for ways to improve his performance and add value to the team.
- A winner always expects to be victorious.
- A winner is not afraid of risk.

Stay in Shape

It is extremely important to stay in shape year-round. Again, take your cue from the pros who work hard in the off-season to stay fit. Whether you decide to concentrate on one sport or participate in other sports is your decision. However, do not become inactive, and don't stay away from your training for more than a few weeks at a time.

Staying in top physical form demonstrates to college coaches that you are serious about your commitment to your sport and your future. Also, it's good for your health and will improve your academic effectiveness.

Become a Leader

Coaches admire athletes who demonstrate a winning attitude, have mental toughness, take charge of workouts, and maintain composure under pressure. Not only will these traits make you a better athlete, but they will help you elevate the ability of your teammates as well. So be a leader, not a follower.

If you're not one of those "verbal types," lead by example with your work ethic in practice and your desire to improve. If you are one of those athletes who likes to talk to your teammates, keep it positive and enthusiastic.

Whatever your personality, strive to be someone who is described by his coach and teammates as a student of the game, a great team player, and a winner.

One coach reveals that he discovers who the leaders are at tryouts by asking who wants to lead the drill they are getting ready to do. The players who jump out and lead the warm-ups, for instance, have just shown they are leaders. Also, the players who try to jump to the head of the line for each drill will stand out as not only leaders but players who are eager about their sport.

> ### Chalk Talk
>
> "I look for athletes with positive attitudes who always hustle. In addition, they must have an inner drive to accomplish things as an individual and on a team level. A leader tries to make those around him better and shows a commitment to doing things right the first time."
>
> —Dan Ireland, Head Track Coach, Yale University, NCAA D-I

Don't be negative! A player who openly criticizes teammates for errors during scrimmages or games or even drills is not the kind of leader coaches are looking for. However, the player who openly and sincerely boosts their teammates' confidence after a miscue is exactly the kind of leader coaches love and want to have on their squads.

Attend Prospect Camps at Your Top Target Schools

Most college coaches run their own camps for high school athletes. These camps are usually one week long and packed with instruction, guest speakers, and informal competition. Many schools host two or more camps in different seasons—namely, winter/summer or spring/fall.

Attending camp is an ideal opportunity to gain exposure with the recruiting staff, get a feel for what these coaches are looking for, and visit the campus. From the coaches' standpoints, they are getting to know you as a person and an athlete, evaluating not only your talent but whether you would be a good fit in their systems.

Academic Suggestions

Before a college coach decides if he is going to recruit you, he looks at your GPA, core courses, and SAT/ACT scores to make sure you meet his school's admission standards. If you are way below the minimum requirements, he will not waste his time recruiting you, regardless of how much you could help his team. Poor grades assure you of only one thing when it comes to college admission and sports: fewer choices.

If you run faster, shoot better, or throw farther than anyone in your league, junior college will be your only option if you are not academically strong enough to be admitted to a four-year school. Even an All-State caliber athlete with a poor track record in the classroom will give a scholarship-equipped coach pause.

Coaches know that athletes who don't perform in class are more likely to become academically ineligible or flunk out at the college level—and that may be more risk than a coach is willing to take. If a coach has only one scholarship left and must choose between two athletes of equal talent, he will always select the better student.

Improve Your Grades, and More Schools Will Be Able to Recruit You

Say, for example, you have a 2.6 GPA and 870 SAT score. While those marks are average, you've automatically taken yourself off the recruiting lists of probably five hundred strong academic schools! Imagine how many more opportunities you will have if you meet the admission requirements of all schools in the country or at least a bigger percentage of them?

Consider that a school you're interested in may have requirements peculiar to that school—you need to be aware of those if they exist. For instance, in California, getting into the top state-sponsored universities (University of California system) requires *very* good grades as well as very specific requirements for high school classes. A biology class you took in your high school in Nebraska may not have the content they require.

Other schools in other states often have similar "extra" requirements. Check out each school you're interested in to make sure the classes you take will qualify. There has been more than one instance of a student-athlete who has graduated from high school with good grades and met all the NCAA Clearinghouse requirements . . . and was still unable to meet the college entrance requirements of a particular school.

While this isn't the norm, it still happens often enough that you need to be prepared, which means you should try to identify as early as possible the schools you're interested in and be aware of the "above and beyond" requirements that you still have time to do something about!

> ### Chalk Talk
>
> "I place very high expectations on academics. That's what you're here for. You go to college to grow as a person and learn some of life's skills. I expect maximum effort in the classroom. Sports will complement that."
>
> —*Marcus O'Sullivan, Head Track Coach, Villanova University, NCAA D-I*

Set high goals for yourself in each class you take. Do not settle for mediocrity. Be disciplined with your homework and strive to reach your full potential. If you're receiving Bs right now, go for As. Ask your teacher for extra help, hire a tutor, form a study group with your friends, or take a preparatory SAT/ACT course. Take advanced placement (AP) classes if you can qualify for them.

Do whatever it takes to improve your academic standing and do not believe for one second that grades are unimportant. Nothing impresses a college coach more than athletes who work just as hard in the classroom as they do on the playing field.

Here's a bit of advice that will just about ensure that you'll be a success not only in athletics and your studies but later on in your vocation, with relationships, and in life in general. Adopt the "10 percent rule." The 10 percent rule is simple. Just do 10 percent extra in everything you do. Whatever is asked of you by your coach, your teacher, your parents, or your supervisor, do just 10 percent more than is required. Try it. You'll be amazed at the results.

Also, try to be the first to arrive at the game or practice or job, and be the last to leave. "Gym rats" are highly prized commodities!

Manage Your Time Effectively

Since your daily schedule is already filled with classes, sports, and extracurricular activities, it's important you set aside a block of time each night for homework and your college search. Make it a priority and be disciplined. You will reap the rewards for many years to come.

Develop Other Interests and Get Involved in Extracurricular Activities

College admissions officers look favorably on students who have multiple interests and are involved in a range of activities. Find an organization at your school (i.e., school newspaper, drama club, band, foreign language club, etc.) that interests you and get involved. Also, you may want to consider volunteering a few hours each month at a local charity or nonprofit organization.

More than one school will take an applicant with a 3.5 GPA who's been involved in extracurricular activities and community service over an applicant with a 4.0 who's done nothing else. A mother in California told us about a classmate of her son's who was her class's valedictorian . . . and was turned down by UCLA and Cal because she didn't have the classes they required and she had no extracurricular activities.

Don't worry about trying to become a Renaissance man or woman at age seventeen. Not many high school seniors are perfect, well-rounded students. Just show a passion for one or two of your strongest interests. Do not simply build a resume that lists every club in your school. What impresses admissions officers is proof that an activity is a theme in your life . . . think quality, not quantity.

> ### Catch This
>
> Recently, a counselor urged one student, a television-sports addict, to get off the couch and get involved. The student started writing a sports column for the high school paper, coaching basketball in a poor neighborhood, and interning at an all-sports television channel.
> The counselor is betting that he'll have several admission offers to choose from next year.

Work to Increase Your GPA

If you did not perform well in your freshman year of high school, you may be given the benefit of the doubt if your grades go up in your sophomore, junior, and senior years. Your goal should be to graduate ranked as high as possible in your class. And by all means, avoid "senioritis." Don't think that you can coast as soon as your applications are finished. Colleges will notice if you drop an AP course, take an easy schedule, or let your GPA slide in your senior year. Some schools will even pull admission offers from a student who performs poorly in his senior year.

Hire a Tutor or Enroll in a SAT/ACT Preparation Course

Ask your guidance counselor for suggestions to raise your college entrance exam scores. Kaplan and Princeton Review offer outstanding courses you may want to consider. Taking a prep course will boost your confidence tremendously. Some students hire private tutors or purchase computer study programs.

If you have to, take these exams several times until you are satisfied with your scores. Regardless of which exams you take, don't assume a higher-than-average score will guarantee acceptance to your dream school. Test scores are not weighted as heavily as most people think they are, although very poor scores can be difficult to overcome. It's just another part of the package.

Take Advanced Placement or College-Level Courses

College admissions officers will view you as a motivated student if your high school transcript features some honors and AP courses. Your GPA may slide a little, but it's worth it to take advanced classes in areas where you are strong.

For example, if you've always received good grades in math, take AP calculus and AP statistics. If writing and reading are your strong points, take AP English. Remember, your transcript is the most important piece of your application. Many admissions officers would rather see you challenge yourself than get straight As in easy courses. Many colleges weight AP classes by scoring them a half-grade higher than regular courses for the student's GPA.

Spend Your Summers Productively

Admissions deans don't look kindly on summers spent relaxing at the beach or on the couch, but otherwise they're surprisingly open-minded. If you need money, take that fast-food restaurant job, and then try to make the experience as meaningful as you can. For example, sign up for a community college course or summer enrichment program, or do volunteer work.

Take Both Entrance Exams

Virtually all colleges accept both the SAT and ACT, so you may want to take them both and just feature the better score on your application. To determine which you'll find easier, take a practice version of each and compare your scores using a concordance table (www.collegeboard.com has one available online).

Finish Line

You've just learned about some of the ways you can improve your profile as you get ready to be a part of the recruiting process. Use the following list to make a note about where you rate in each of these areas and where you'd like to be. If it's an area that needs improvement, highlight it so that you can focus your plan to improve.

Athletic	Excellent	Average	Needs work	Goal
Leadership	☐	☐	☐	_____
Endurance	☐	☐	☐	_____
Foot speed	☐	☐	☐	_____
Strength	☐	☐	☐	_____
Flexibility	☐	☐	☐	_____
Attitude	☐	☐	☐	_____
Practice habits	☐	☐	☐	_____
Relationship w/coach	☐	☐	☐	_____
Relationship w/team	☐	☐	☐	_____

Nonathletic

	Excellent	Average	Needs work	Goal
Grades	☐	☐	☐	_____
SAT/ACT scores	☐	☐	☐	_____
Time management	☐	☐	☐	_____
Work ethic	☐	☐	☐	_____
Attitude	☐	☐	☐	_____
Leadership	☐	☐	☐	_____

Your College Lineup

In this chapter:

- ☐ How to rank schools by academic factors
- ☐ Making sure you will like the campus life
- ☐ Reasons to target certain schools
- ☐ What to look for in the athletic program
- ☐ How to cross-reference your athletic and academic needs and desires

To become the focus of a college coach on the hunt for new athletes, you've got to work hard to make him aware of who you are and what you can do. This chapter is about another step in the recruiting process: doing the research and investigation required to create a Target List of schools that meet your academic and athletic needs. From your Target List, there will be five to ten schools you will apply to and one that you may ultimately attend. Coaches from these schools will hear from you and evaluate you at their camps and showcases—and, hopefully, your high school coach and guidance counselors will reach out to them as well. Ironically, at the beginning of this process, it's you who will be doing the recruiting of the college coach you want to compete for.

Creating Your Target List

Step 1: Who Are You?

Let's start by trying to identify the schools that interest you for academic and personal growth reasons. Why start with academics? Because chances are, like 99 percent of all other college-bound high school athletes, you may not have the good fortune of earning a living as a professional athlete.

At the end of your college career, you will leave campus with at least three priceless assets: great memories of college sports, friends you will have for life, and a diploma. After you've thrown your last pitch, run your last race, or scored your last goal, your degree and the education it represents will be your ticket into the career of your choice and the beginning of your adult life.

We think the best way to begin evaluating schools is to first evaluate yourself. Once you know your own strengths and weaknesses academically, personally, and athletically, it will be much easier to match yourself with different colleges. Take out a paper and pen and describe yourself according to these categories:

- Academic likes and dislikes: Which subjects do you enjoy the most? What do you want to learn more about? What have you excelled at to date?
- Extracurricular: Which recreational activities, community services, and religious activities do you currently participate in and hope to continue in college?
- Personality traits: Are you shy or outgoing? Independent or more comfortable in a structured environment? Want to be far from home or within driving distance? Hang out with different kinds of people?

As we said earlier, the question "What's the best college for me?" is a multiple-choice question with more than one right answer. What we are trying to help you to do is divide the enormous pie of American colleges into manageable slices, creating boundary lines between broad categories of schools. As long as you focus

Catch This

If you want a great online resource for college searching, *U.S. News & World Report* (www.usnews.com) offers a fabulous search engine that you should definitely explore.

on the slice with schools that feel right for you, a good choice will be made no matter which school you ultimately select.

Say, for example, you want a medium-sized school with a suburban campus, within driving distance from home, a strong business faculty, and a competitive Division II team. There may be up to a dozen schools that fit this criteria, and the differences among them will be much less significant than say, the difference between a big state university and any institution in your target group.

Once you have written down as much information about yourself as possible, it's time to begin looking at schools and learning about which ones look promising and which ones you can eliminate from consideration. The following factors are ones we think work best to quickly screen colleges and enable you to come up with a small but reasonably diverse list of schools that you can then attempt to visit or research in greater depth.

Factor 1: Location, Location, Location

Just like in real estate, location is an important consideration when trying to whittle down a list of colleges from hundreds to dozens. Schools are either "nearby," "within driving distance," or "a plane ride away." The closer to home you wish to be, the more schools you can cross off your consideration list. Conversely, if you have no preference about distance from home or being far away, then location is less of an issue for you.

Work with your parents on this one because where you go to school obviously has a big effect on how often you will see your family over the next four years and how often they will see you. There's also a cost element to consider, as getting to and from school can be hundreds or thousands of dollars a year, much more than the cost of a tank of gas.

Likewise, do you want to be in a rural, suburban, or urban setting? On the walk from your dorm to the library, will you encounter shattered glass and boarded-up buildings or ivy-clad brick buildings and broad expanses of green?

During your downtime, will you go snowboarding or snorkeling, apple picking or clothes shopping? Many students also underestimate how strongly the weather can affect their spirits and ability to succeed. If you live in a warm Southern climate, love the beach, and have never skied before, make sure you understand that going to college in places such as New York, Boston, or Chicago will require a rather significant lifestyle adjustment.

Factor 2: Size Matters

The size of a school—how many students and square miles of campus—will also influence the quality of your college experience. Big schools with tens of thousands of students are almost like medium-sized cities unto themselves. Do you want to walk to class or take a shuttle bus? Be able to meet in person with your professors after class just to get an e-mail correspondence going? Choose from hundreds of clubs and organizations to join (for example, there are nine hundred clubs and organizations at the University of Wisconsin–Madison)?

> ### Catch This
>
> You should also keep in mind that local companies tend to recruit on campuses, leading many graduates to settle in the area where they attended college. So quite often your choice of a college affects the region you settle in for good, not just for four years.

The advantages of a big school are many—incredible academic and extracurricular choices, lots of different people from different places to meet and befriend, and well-financed athletic teams and facilities.

Depending on your personality, however, you may find these pluses don't outweigh your concerns about large class sizes, the impersonal nature of such a large community, and having to interact with the bureaucracy that manages today's big modern university.

Smaller schools, on the other hand, typically have smaller classes, a more intimate social environment, and a generally more accessible administration. Combine your size and location preferences and you probably have made a great start toward narrowing the list of schools you want to spend time researching further.

Factor 3: Majors Are Minor Issues, for Now

What do you want to major in? It may be the most popular question put to college-bound high schoolers as they enter application season. While it's fine, perhaps even an advantage, to know what you want to major in at college, it's also perfectly fine to be undecided. So why bring it up here? Well, if you're one of those young people who knows exactly what he wants to study—engineering, hotel and restaurant management, or agricultural science, for example—you certainly will have an easier time creating a list of colleges to focus on.

If you're the opposite type and have no idea what you want to major in, then you probably would want to avoid the specialty schools, which means you, too, can narrow your list. For students in between, who can't specify what they do or don't want to study, don't worry. Most students arrive at school with one major in mind and then decide to switch, sometimes as late as their junior year of college. If you aren't sure what direction to take, just concentrate on schools with lots of options. It's okay to be flexible in life and in college majors!

Factor 4: Campus Culture

You will do your best academically if you feel as though you fit in on campus. Reflect on your social life in high school. Are you looking for a school that offers more diversity? Less? Do you want to spend your nights at film festivals, frat parties, or focusing on studies?

During your campus visits, take some time to observe the student body and see how they interact with each other. If you get a chance to talk to students on campus, ask how people with different backgrounds and interests get along. College is an amazing place where you will grow emotionally and intellectually by leaps and bounds.

You will have fantastic new experiences in class, with friends, and in athletics. Only you know which kind of environment suits you best, so be honest with yourself and try to steer toward settings that match your comfort zone while still holding out the promise of exciting challenges and opportunities.

Factor 5: Social and Academic Freedom

Question: Do you want to go to a college where students are treated as adults, where they make their own decisions about where to live and which classes to take, and where they are graded on just midterm and final exams? Tired of following rules and schedules set by their parents, many college-bound high schoolers would answer with an emphatic *Yes!*

Well, be careful, because it's a tricky question. Sudden immersion into a life with few rules isn't always easy. For one thing, if you have freedom, so does everybody else—including the kids who are carousing outside your door the night before your chemistry midterm. Are you the kind of person who is easily influenced by your friends? If the honest answer is yes, then a school with too few rules or a big school where it's easy to get lost in the shuffle may be the wrong place for you.

Colleges differ widely on the matter of how much freedom they grant undergrads. Some schools have lots of detailed rules, such as class attendance requirements, designated residential facilities, and restrictions on parties, whereas others are very hands-off, except in cases of extreme behavior, such as plagiarism, cheating, or threats to others.

Having thought about whether you would blossom or flounder in an unstructured environment is a really important element in the college selection process. Remember, whichever path you choose, you will meet hundreds or thousands of young adults who feel the same as you. It would be a shame to arrive at school as a freshman and suddenly discover that you hadn't considered this particular issue carefully enough and were out of sync with your new classmates.

Factor 6: Religion

This is kind of a subset of factors 4 and 5 because there are many colleges in America where religion is a central element to campus life, and that obviously influences the cultural and academic environment. If you know you want to attend a college with a Catholic, Jesuit, Mormon, or Jewish culture, for example, your choices are easily narrowed to fine institutions such as Notre Dame, Loyola, Boston College, Brigham Young, and Brandeis.

If you want the kind of structural, social, and cultural trappings that come with an academic institution that identifies with a particular religion, you are fortunate enough to live in a country where these choices are both available and plentiful. Just do your homework on the schools you are looking at so you know what to expect.

Factor 7: Diversity

Many colleges, particularly private ones, are making a concerted effort to attract minority students in increasing numbers. If you're going to be a success in the twenty-first century, you must be capable of understanding and dealing with individuals whose backgrounds are different from yours. It will also make you a better human being.

Guidance counselors caution students to look at more than statistics when considering diversity. They suggest you consider whether the curriculum embraces other traditions and whether residence halls tend to be integrated or segregated. For schools where the commitment to diversity is made in earnest, the opportunity for you to acquire a deeper understanding of others can be a large reward.

Factor 8: Academic Qualifications

If you are a C student with combined SATs below 1000, there are many schools you will not qualify for academically, so just scratch them from your list and move on. Not everyone can go to an Ivy League school, and not every Ivy League graduate is a success in the adult world. Our point is simple and obvious: Be optimistic, but also be realistic.

Take into account the minimum academic performance each school is looking for, before you put them on your Target List. This is one of those cold realities of the college selection process. While its fine to have a couple of schools on your Target List that would be considered "stretches," make sure you also end up with schools where you are well within the range of their academic requirements.

We've listed eight factors that we believe can help you quickly and effectively narrow a huge pool of schools to a Target List of a dozen or so colleges: a group small enough for you to research each institution individually and put them all in order of preference. Next is step 2, where you'll need to evaluate the athletic side of the table to see which of the schools on your Target List suit your sports needs.

How Some Schools Stack Up

Aside from choosing a school to compete at, you are also choosing a new home. It is important that you are comfortable with all aspects of life on campus. Some criteria to consider include the following: best value, best academic facilities, best freshman housing, biggest party school, and what's hot and trendy. Here are how some schools stack up, in no particular order, according to Kaplan's book *The Unofficial, Biased, Insider's Guide to the 320 Most Interesting Colleges*. To order your copy, call 1-800-KAP-TEST or go to www.kaptest.com.

Best Value

U. of Arizona, AZ
Harvard U., MA
Penn State U., PA
Rice U., TX
Yale U., CT
Rutgers U., NJ
U. of Washington, WA
U. of Maryland, MD
U. of Colorado, CO
U. of Notre Dame, IN
U. of Wisconsin, WI
Berea C., KY
U. of California, CA
Virginia Poly & S. U., VA
U. of Virginia, VA
Washington U., MO
West Virginia U., WV
U. of Kansas, KS
Duke U., NC
U. of North Carolina, NC
U. of Michigan, MI
C. of New Jersey, NJ
Miami U., OH
Oklahoma State U., OK
Texas Tech U., TX
U. of Minnesota, MN
U. of Missouri, MO
Purdue U., IN
U. of Nebraska, NE
Truman State U., MO
U. of Texas, TX
James Madison U., VA
Cornell U., NY
Stanford U., CA
U. of Delaware, DE
Texas A & M U., TX
Northwestern U., IL
Grove City C., PA
Tulane U., LA

Best Academic Facilities

U. of California, CA
Stanford U., CA
Texas A & M U., TX
U. of Texas-Austin, TX
U. of Illinois-Urbana, IL
Harvard U., MA
U. of California, CA
New York U., NY
Penn State U., PA
California Inst. of Tech., CA
Georgia Inst. of Tech., GA
Mass Inst. of Tech., MA
Ohio State U., OH
California Poly State U., CA
Princeton U., NJ
Rice U., TX
Virginia Poly Inst. & S. U., VA
U. of Houston, TX
U. of Rochester, NY
Cornell U., NY
Duke U., NC
North Carolina State U., NC
U. of Michigan, MI
U. of Kentucky, KY
Rochester Inst. of Tech., NY
U. of Missouri, MO
U. of Wisconsin, WI
U. of Chicago, IL
U. of Central Florida, FL
Pittsburgh State U., PA
U. of Virginia, VA
U. of Notre Dame, IN
U. of North Carolina, NC
U. of Florida, FL
U. of Georgia, GA
Michigan State U., MI
Carnegie Mellon U., PA
Pepperdine U., CA
U. of Utah, UT
Dartmouth C., NH
Northern Michigan U., MI
Brigham Young U., UT

Best Freshman Housing

Texas A & M U., TX
U. of California, CA
Stanford U., CA
Illinois Wesleyan U., IL
Penn State U., PA
Stephan F. Austin State U., TX
U. of Texas, TX
New York U., NY
U. of Central Florida, FL
Florida State U., FL
U. of California, CA
Texas Tech U., TX
Rice U., TX
U. of Illinois-Urbana, IL
Indiana U. of Pennsylvania, PA
Miami U., FL
Michigan State, MI
Wright State, OH
Kent State, OH
U. of Utah, UT
Ball State U., IN
Stonehill C., MA
Marshall U., WV
Washington State U., WA
Grand Valley State U., MI
Oklahoma State U., OK
U. of North Carolina, NC

Best Party Schools

California State U., CA
San Jose State U., CA
U. of Florida, FL
Southwest Texas State U., TX
U. of Texas, TX
Southern Illinois U., IL
Florida State U., FL
West Virginia U., WV
Ohio U., OH
U. of Miami, MI
Bloomsberg U. of Penn., PA
U. of Wisconsin, WI
Penn State U., PA
Washington State U., WA
U. of Georgia, GA
Saint Cloud State U., MN
U. of Virginia, VA
U. of Wisconsin, WI
East Carolina U., NC
U. of Missouri, MO

Hot and Trendy

Harvard U., MA
U. of North Carolina, NC
Duke U., NC
New York U., NY
U. of California, CA
Georgetown U., DC
U. of Colorado, CO
Brown U., RI
U. of Maryland, MD
Princeton U., NJ
Boston C., MA
Stanford U., CA
U. of Arizona, AZ
U. of Texas-Austin, TX
Boston U., MA
Wash. U. Saint Louis, MO
Texas A & M U., TX
Arizona State U., AZ
U. of Virginia, VA
U. of Wisconsin, WI
Mass Inst. of Tech., MA
San Diego State U., CA
Virginia Poly Inst., & S. U., VA
George Washington U., DC
Florida State U., FL
U. of California, CA
U. of Southern California, CA
Penn State U., PA
Pepperdine U., CA
U. of Florida, FL
U. of Miami, FL

Step 2: Will I Contribute?

Step 2 is to take your Target List and research each school's athletic program. Try to place them in an order based on whether you think you have an opportunity to make the team and be a contributor. At the top of this list would be schools where you believe you could step right in and play your freshman year. At the bottom of the list would be the schools where you're not sure you would even make the team.

Make sure that you visit www.collegecoachesonline.com every few months and search for schools that meet your criteria. This is an extremely valuable resource that you definitely want to use. A free one-year subscription is included with this guide. E-mail info@collegeboundsports.com if you misplace your login password.

Focus on Schools Where You Can Be a Contributing Athlete

We think it's worth repeating: The most important sports factor to consider in prioritizing your Target List is the likelihood of playing. Since it could be unlikely that you will be a professional athlete, what's the point of spending your last four years in the game never coming off the bench? Instead, play the sport you love at a school where you will also receive a solid education.

Be Prepared to Play in Any Division

It's a good idea to include schools from every division (NCAA, NAIA, and NJCAA) on your Target List. Don't get hung up on Division I schools. There are schools at every level that can meet your athletic and education needs.

Honestly Assess Your Athletic Ability

- How have you performed at major events, such as showcases, tournaments, meets, and state or national championships?
- Do you know any college athletes with abilities similar to yours?
- Do you possess impressive physical attributes? A coach may recruit you if he believes that you can develop into a great athlete over the next two to three years.
- Do you possess the leadership ability necessary to compete in college?
- Do you play for competitive summer or club leagues?

Keep in mind that you may compare yourself to the athletes on your team, in your league, or among those with whom you consider yourself a top recruit. Meanwhile, coaches scout not only those same athletes but thousands more throughout the country. That's why it's important to attend camps and tournaments outside your region.

This reality check is not meant to destroy your dream, just alter it enough to make it more attainable. Remember that each school's needs can change from year to year. Priorities can change because of graduation, injuries, transfers, sub-par performances, or academic suspensions. There is a match for you somewhere in the country. Keep an open mind and do not neglect a school simply because of its name.

Hit the Web

Check out the media guides or webpages of your Target List schools. This will give you a feel for how important the athletic department is within the school's hierarchy and how important your sport is within the athletic department.

Hopefully, the school's website will also tell you about the coaches, facilities, and conference the school competes in. You should also check out the biography of each player on the roster. It's a pretty good indicator of whether the coach recruits athletes like you.

Take into account the following:

Ability: If you notice that most athletes on a team were state champions and you've only been awarded Second Team All-League, that's a pretty good indicator that the talent level may be too high for you.

Physical characteristics: How does your height and weight measure up other players on the team?

Geography: Does the coach recruit nationally or regionally, or is he satisfied with the in-state talent? Where are most of the athletes from?

Position: Is the team already stocked at your position? This may be an indication that they have a great program for that position. However, it also may mean that they recruit the position heavily, and thus it may take a couple of years before you are good enough to play.

Years of eligibility: Do they expect everyone to graduate in four years? Does the conference allow graduate students to compete in their conference?

Junior college transfers: Does the coach recruit JUCO transfers, who generally are more experienced and better athletes than high school graduates?

Overstocking players: Some coaches purposely overrecruit players by position so that they can "cherry-pick" from the surplus. A coach who does this may call the "extra" players into his office and "gently" urge them to consider enrolling at a JUCO until a spot opens up for them. This is a situation that is actually becoming more and more common.

Case Study: How One Player Used Athletic Team Webpages to Evaluate Schools for His Target List

Here is how one fictional player—Jason Kline—used the web to compare schools on his Target List. Using his physical attributes and high school statistics, he examined how he fit into two collegiate baseball programs. Take a similar approach with your search, no matter what sport you aspire to play.

Personal Info

Name:	Jason Kline
Height:	5-8
Weight:	150
Position:	SS
B/T:	R/R
Graduation:	2005
Hometown:	Yorktown Heights, NY
School:	Yorktown High School

Continued

2004 Stats

AVG	GP	AB	R	H	2B	3B	HR	RBI	BB	SO
.325	31	114	28	37	13	4	6	24	14	9

Bio

Jason is an outstanding shortstop entering his second full season on the varsity squad at Yorktown High School. Last year as a junior, Jason led the team in average (.325) and hits (37) and was second in RBI (24). He also led the team in fielding percentage (.977), committing just 1 error in 44 chances at short. Named team captain for his senior year, Jason will make a run at a second consecutive All-Section honor in Westchester County.

Goals

Upon graduation, Jason wants to play for a Division I program on the East Coast. He wants the opportunity to start at shortstop and have an immediate impact his freshman year. With this in mind, he's narrowed his Target List down to two schools. Always enamored by the Florida State program, Jason grew up watching the Seminoles compete on television, and he's aware of his father's success as the FSU third baseman ('71–'75). He would relish the opportunity to continue his father's legacy in an established collegiate baseball program.

He is also considering Quinnipiac University, a smaller institution located in Connecticut. Quinnipiac is entering its fifth season as a Division I program, and Jason sees this as a good place to bring his leadership qualities and grow with the program. Although the schools offer completely different options, Jason sees advantages to each and is ready to hit the web.

Florida State University's Baseball Roster

Overall record: 54–11–1   **League record: 19–5**

National ranking: #1

Head coach: Mike Martin

No.	Name	Pos	B/T	HT	WT	YR	Hometown
1	Tony McQuade	OF	S-R	6-2	205	SO	Gainesville, FL
2	Rocky Roquet	OF	R-R	6-2	195	FR	Anaheim, CA
4	Stephen Drew	SS	L-R	6-0	175	FR	Hahira, GA
5	Jerrod Brown	1B	L-R	5-10	200	JR	Auburndale, FL

No.	Name	Pos	B/T	HT	WT	YR	Hometown
7	Daniel Hodges	P	L-L	6-0	180	JR	Hilliard, FL
8	Michael Futrell	OF	R-R	6-0	180	SR	Tallahassee, FL
9	Kevin Richman	SS	S-R	6-0	160	FR	Clearwater, FL
10	Chris Hart	1B	S-R	6-1	190	JR	Clearwater, FL
13	Justin Miller	P	L-L	5-9	150	FR	Quincy, FL
14	Bryan Zech	2B	R-R	5-10	175	SO	Wellington, FL
15	Jeff Probst	2B-SS	R-R	5-10	175	SO	Clearwater, FL
16	Scott Toole	2B-3B	R-R	6-1	185	SR	Jacksonville, FL
17	Chris Whidden	P	R-R	6-0	175	JR	Tallahassee, FL
18	D. Davidson	P	L-L	6-4	215	JR	Panama City, FL
19	A. Cheesman	C	R-R	5-10	190	FR	Sarasota, FL
20	Robinson	OF	R-R	6-1	190	FR	D. Bar, CA
21	Blair Varnes	P	R-R	6-2	200	SR	Pascagoula, MS
22	Jason Newlin	P	R-R	6-0	185	JR	Tallahassee, FL
23	Tony Richie	C	R-R	6-1	210	SO	Jacksonville, FL
24	Eric Roman	P	R-R	6-2	195	JR	Orlando, FL
25	Nick Rogers	OF	R-R	6-1	195	SR	Vedra Beach, FL
26	Kevin Lynch	P-3B	L-R	6-2	185	FR	Ft. Pierce, FL
27	R. Barthelemy	3B-1B	L-R	6-3	230	SR	Miami, FL
29	Richie Smith	OF	L-R	5-11	200	SR	Bristol, FL
30	Robby Read	P	R-R	6-2	195	JR	Tallahassee, FL
31	M. LaMacchia	P	R-R	6-0	190	SO	Palm Harbor, FL
32	Blair McCaleb	C	R-R	6-0	205	SR	Marietta, GA
35	Brent Marsh	P	R-R	6-3	185	FR	Tallahassee, FL
42	Tommy Stewart	OF	R-R	6-2	225	JR	Largo, FL
43	Trent Peterson	P	R-L	6-1	180	SO	Tallahassee, FL
46	Matt Lynch	P	L-L	6-2	185	JR	Ft. Pierce, FL

Relevant numbers

31 players on roster

8 freshman

6 sophomores

10 juniors

7 seniors

6 of the freshman are position players, 2 pitchers

25 are from Florida

3 SS on roster: (2 freshman, 1 sophomore)

Consider Jason's evaluation of Florida State. Remember, this is based on his profile and goals. You may have a different outlook.

Continued

Things to consider . . .

- Nationally recognized as one of country's top programs.
- Incredible facilities, fields, road trips, and so forth.
- 3 SS on the roster—all are freshman and sophomores, so I'd probably need to change positions to have a chance at seeing time.
- Coach recruits primarily from Florida—very few out-of-staters on roster.
- Will have to compete against some of country's top players for a roster spot.
- All players on roster have more accolades than I do.
- All players on roster are taller and heavier than I am.
- Will most likely have to make team as a walk-on.
- Too far for parents and friends to attend my games.
- Would be a dream to experience College World Series and be on ESPN.

Quinnipiac University Baseball Roster

Overall record: 17–24

League record: 14–13

National ranking: #278

Head coach: Dan Gooley

No.	Name	Ht/Wt	Pos	B/T	YR	Hometown
1	Avery, Keith	5-10/170	OF	R/R	JR	Trumbull, CT
2	D'Elia, Charles	5-11/165	SS	R/R	SR	Neponset, NY
3	Bennett, Dave	6-0/170	P	R/R	SO	Fairfield, CT
4	Puccio, Sal	6-1/205	1B/3B	R/R	SR	Brightwaters, NY
5	Jasilli, John	5-11/155	IF/P	R/R	SR	Brooklyn, NY
7	Marano, Albert	5-10/170	OF	R/R	SO	Lincoln, RI
8	Zides, Andy	5-8/175	INF	R/R	JR	Canton, MA
9	Silverstein, St.	5-8/160	C	R/R	SO	Merrick, NY
10	Bengel, Richard	5-11/175	P	L/L	SO	New Bern, NC
11	Abrahams, Dan	5-7/140	OF	R/R	SO	Great Neck, NY
13	Melillo, John	5-10/190	P	R/R	JR	Wethersfield, CT
14	Garrett, Robert	6-2/200	C/1B	R/R	JR	Brookfield, CT
19	Magee, Brian	6-2/200	OF	L/R	SR	Stamford, CT
20	Spahr, Mike	6-2/205	P	R/R	FR	Oceanport, NJ
21	LaPointe, T.	6-0/190	IF	R/R	JR	West Haven, CT
24	Rankowitz, K.	6-0/185	C	R/R	SO	Barrington, RI

No.	Name	Ht/Wt	Pos	B/T	YR	Hometown
25	Stonaha, Chris	6-0/175	3B	R/R	SO	Stratford, CT
30	Lavigne, Seth	6-3/240	OF	R/R	JR	Tolland, CT
31	Kafka, Ari	6-5/215	P	R/R	FR	Sharon, MA
32	Ellis, Jackson	6-1/190	P	R/R	JR	Ludlow, VT
33	Vartuli, Chris	6-0/190	C	R/R	SO	Norwalk, CT
36	Gresh, Chris	6-1/220	P	R/R	FR	Jewett City, CT

Relevant numbers

22 players on roster

3 freshman

8 sophomores

7 juniors

4 seniors

All 3 freshman are pitchers

15 are from NY/CT/NJ

1 SS on roster (a senior)

Consider Jason's evaluation of Quinnipiac. Remember, this is based on his profile and goals. You may have a different outlook.

Things to consider . . .

- Not known for baseball program.
- Coach recruits from the Northeast.
- Small school, less pressure.
- 1 SS on the roster and he's graduating.
- Good chance of seeing a lot of time freshman year.
- Players on roster have fewer accolades that are more in-line with mine.
- Less competition for a starting position.
- Average player on roster is roughly my size.
- School is closer to home, so family and friends can watch me play.
- No freshman position players on roster—may have to wait until sophomore year to start
- All three freshmen on the team are pitchers.
- Smaller roster means fewer spots available, fewer scouts, fewer road trips, and so on.
- Cold weather climate—can't play outside year-round.

Continued

Final Analysis

You can learn a lot about how you fit in with a particular program just by evaluating their roster online. However, a roster from one particular year is not proof of a trend, and some media guides inflate the accomplishments of their athletes to make their program appear more prestigious.

As always, the bottom line is that there is no substitute for going the extra step after your initial research is done. Reach out to coaches, athletes, and recent graduates, and search the web for results of tournaments and conference championships. Be as knowledgeable as possible on each college you are considering applying to.

Watch for Red Flags

You need to be aware of a couple of red flags when investigating athletic programs of schools on your Target List. If you notice a team you're interested in has only a few juniors and seniors on the roster, inquire about the following:

- How many athletes compete all four years?
- Do many quit after their first or second seasons?
- How many athletes receive diplomas?
- Do athletes suffer an unusually high number of injuries?

Step 3: Finalize Your List

You now should have two versions of your Target List, one with schools in order of academic preference and the other in order of athletic preference. See if you can combine the two lists without dramatically changing the order of either one. If one or more of the schools are in the top ten of both lists, you've got yourself a great indicator of which schools you should focus on applying and gaining admission to.

Finish Line

Okay, you now know how to do it, so it's time to build those lists. Using the information in this chapter and the information from the previous chapters as well, begin to build your lists of schools based on academics and athletics. Then, compare the two lists, and you've begun to target schools that are a good all-around match for you.

Academic Schools	Athletic Schools

CHAPTER 5

Essential Action Steps to Take

In this chapter:

☐ Different ways to promote yourself

☐ How and when to make campus visits

☐ Information on recruiting services

☐ When it's a good idea to try out as a walk-on

So far in this guide, you've learned how college coaches look at the recruiting process, where you can get help, how to improve your profile to generate interest, and how to make a Target List of colleges you might want to attend. Now, it's time to take action. This chapter covers a variety of steps that you can take to make sure that college coaches at your Target List schools are aware of you and take an interest in you and that, as a result, your chances increase of your being admitted to the schools of your choice.

Promoting Yourself

Apply to Strong Academic Schools

As you might suspect, college coaches frequently work with admissions officers to get student-athletes admitted who might not otherwise qualify academically or are "on the bubble." Of course, this does not mean that a student whose academic profile is significantly below the school's minimums will be accepted simply at the coach's request.

However, if you are within a reasonable distance of a school's SAT/ACT and grade requirements and are an athlete that the coach is seeking to add to his squad, the coach probably has a good shot at getting you into his school if he pushes hard enough.

At some schools, admission requirements may not be as stringent for recruits as they are for nonathletes. An Ivy League school may require students to possess at least a 3.6 GPA and 1400 SAT score, yet a sought-after athletic recruit may only need to have a 3.3 GPA and 1100 SAT.

Remember, coaches at strong academic schools seek good athletes just as their counterparts at the top D-I programs do. Their sports programs have every bit as much tradition and history, sometimes even more than the big D-I schools. And when you graduate, you have an excellent chance of obtaining a great job or being admitted to a graduate school of your choice.

Also, you have a much better chance of competing in college athletics by being a big fish in a small pond if you include some smaller or low-profile schools on your list. For example, if your Target List features the University of Florida (a national D-I powerhouse), where thousands of athletes may apply, and the College of William and Mary (a lesser-known school with an excellent athletic program and academics), where hundreds of athletes may apply, which school do you think gives you a better chance of getting noticed? It's obvious—the statistics favor you at the smaller school.

The bottom line: Use the athletic talents you have worked so hard to develop to give yourself a shot at getting accepted to one of the academic "reach" schools on your Target List. You owe it to yourself to pursue the best possible academic education available.

Let Coaches Know You're Interested

During your junior year, send a letter of interest to each head coach on your Target List. The purpose of the letter of interest is to let each coach know that you would like to attend his school for academic reasons and to compete for his team.

It is extremely important to personalize your letter of interest. If your writing is neat, you might get even more mileage out of a handwritten letter. Make sure you spell the coach's name and address correctly, and include something specific about his team (i.e., team's record, top rivals, great facilities) so he knows your interest is based on knowing something about his program.

One cardinal rule: Whether your letter is handwritten or printed from a computer, do not send a coach a photocopied letter. How do you feel when you get one of those letters that pretends to be written to just you, when it's obvious that same letter has also been sent to thousands of other people?

Catch This

If you're not sure how to write your letter of interest or player profile, see the samples in chapter 7.

You feel as though the sender has no idea who you are and doesn't really care, right? You want a coach to understand that you have genuine and specific interest in his school and that you have devoted a lot of time to researching his program. So make each letter of interest an original, from start to finish!

Begin the letter by explaining your interest in the school's academic program. Mention the major you will pursue or ones you are interested in learning about. Perhaps the school boasts some famous professors whose classes you'd like to attend or famous graduates who had similar interests to yours.

Discuss your educational and career goals, leadership ability, and personal values. These characteristics demonstrate to the coach that you are a well-rounded person and that you plan on staying in school all four years. Avoid the temptation to discuss only athletics in your letter. Coaches are impressed by athletes who treat academics just as seriously as sports.

But don't forget to emphasize your athletic accomplishments and why you feel you can contribute to the team.

- Let the coach know that you have a video available if he would like to see you in action.
- Do not send your tape unless a coach specifically asks for it.
- Request literature about the college, a media guide, any camps they may offer, and a schedule.
- Mention you'd like to come watch a home game.

Along with your letter of interest, you should also provide your personal statistics, which are discussed in the following section, and a copy of your high school schedule, in case the coach decides to send a recruiter to one of your games. Limit your letter of interest to one page (not including the schedule or profile) because coaches are busy people.

Write Your Player Profile

In addition to your upcoming schedule, you should also include a player profile of yourself with each letter of interest you send. This one-page resume should contain personal information, such as your interests, jobs, and volunteer or community work, as well as highlights of your academic and athletic accomplishments. See chapter 7 for details about what items you should include in your player profile.

Telephone and E-mail Contact

After you mail your letter of interest and player profile to coaches on your Target List, it is important for you to maintain periodic telephone or e-mail contact with the school's athletic department. This will let the coach know that your interest is strong and sincere. It will also give you an opportunity to evaluate where you stand on the recruiting depth chart.

Make sure you have a purpose to each contact with a coach or school. For example, you can inform the coach of an event you are attending, ask questions about the program, or request information about the school that cannot be found from published sources. Remember, it is illegal for NCAA coaches to call you or to return your phone calls until the July 1 before your senior year; however, they can e-mail you anytime.

You are permitted to phone and e-mail the coach as many times as you like. Just use common sense. The last thing you want to do is annoy a coach by calling or e-mailing too often. One last bit of advice . . . you should place the phone calls, not your parents. This will demonstrate that you are a mature and responsible young adult who can speak on his or her own behalf.

Develop Your Own Website

Once you are a high school junior, you should publish a personal website to give college coaches an easy and informative way to learn about you and follow your results. It provides recruiters with a free and immediate way of viewing your biography, references, grades and SAT scores, personal statistics, workouts, and even training log.

If you haven't already done so, make sure to set up your free personal website that you received with this guide. Simply visit www.varsitypages.com, enter your unique promo code, and follow the setup directions.

Go to the webpage of each school on your Target List to find the e-mail addresses of the head coach and assistant coaches (some schools have as many as four different coaches and an administrative assistant who handles recruiting). Then e-mail each coach with a link to your website and invite the coach to visit it periodically. Make sure to update your site frequently to encourage repeat traffic.

You can find their e-mail addresses using the free subscription you received with this guide to www.collegecoachesonline.com. You first need to login with your personal username and password.

Ideas to Improve Your Personal Webpage

- Keep the design and layout simple and easy to use. Don't make the coach work too hard to find the necessary information.
- Keep it to one page. Coaches are pressed for time, and too much navigating will discourage them from visiting.
- Include both academic and athletic information.
- Update the site regularly to keep it current—at least once a week during your season.
- Include at least one picture of you in full uniform or an action shot.
- If you have the ability to include a short video clip, do it.
- Don't worry too much about fancy graphics. The coach will visit to get information, not be entertained.
- Make sure your results, personal statistics, height and weight, and any other information you provide are accurate.
- Make sure there are no spelling or grammatical errors.
- Don't forget to e-mail coaches to let them know the page is there!

Press Clippings and Awards

Encourage your high school and summer league or club coaches to submit results and photos to all newspapers in your area. If they don't have the time to do this, ask if you could help out by doing it yourself. When you are mentioned in a newspaper, cut out the article and paste it on a sheet of paper with the newspaper's masthead (name of the paper and publication date found on the front page).

Make enough photocopies for all the schools on your Target List and then go through each article with a yellow marker to highlight wherever your name appears. This will allow the coach to learn about your accomplishments quickly and easily.

Then send the article to the coaches at each Target List school with a handwritten cover note saying, "Dear Coach [insert name], I thought you might be interested in seeing this story. I look forward to speaking with you soon."

Questionnaires

Once a coach knows you're interested in his program from your letter of interest, three important things will happen:

- Your name will be entered in the team's recruiting database.
- You will receive a questionnaire from the coach.
- You will also receive the materials you requested.

The literature you receive will help you learn more about the school and its program and decide whether to keep the school on your Target List.

When your questionnaire arrives, complete it honestly. Avoid the temptation to exaggerate your academic or athletic accomplishments. If a coach discovers inconsistencies, he will remove your name from his recruiting list. Also, let the coach know you are serious about his school by returning the questionnaire as soon as possible. Do not put it off!

Avoid Rushing to Judgment

Do not reject a school too early in the process. Wait until you have thoroughly researched all of your options before telling a coach that you are or are not interested in his school. It's difficult to predict how the recruiting process will evolve, and an offer you turned down in August may be your best or only option in April.

Fill out and return everything! If a coach makes the effort to contact you, respond promptly. Don't burn any bridges.

Emphasize Your Unique Selling Point

Although they hate to admit it, many selective colleges target certain groups of applicants for admission. They might want to increase the diversity of the student body, expand the physics department, or recruit a few potential future donors. To have the freshmen community they want, colleges need musicians and

athletes, leaders in publications and student government, a certain percentage of alumni children, minorities, and international students.

Students in the targeted groups may have an easier time getting through the admission process, and there is often special scholarship money available for people who are from certain backgrounds or are interested in specific programs. You should emphasize what is unique about you.

Hold Up
Avoid the temptation to let your parents complete your questionnaires. If a coach notices an adult's handwriting or language on your form, he will assume you lack maturity and responsibility and that your parents want the opportunity more than you do.

Prove How Badly You Want to Attend the School

Every time you visit a campus, meet an alumnus, or e-mail a professor, let the admissions office know. By rejecting students who have failed to show genuine interest, colleges can boost the percentage of accepted applicants who enroll. A high percentage of accepted applicants who enroll makes schools appear more attractive, and it saves the cost of recruiting students and of "wooing" desirable students with generous merit aid.

A Strong Essay Can Make the Difference

Admissions deans often push hard for the writers of their favorite compositions. However, they also note the papers that are riddled with typos or grammatical errors. Generally speaking, typos reflect sloppiness. Even if you do have a tendency to be light on the spell-check key, there is no excuse for these kinds of errors. They can be eliminated entirely by careful and repetitive proofreading. Eliminate the mistakes and show you care about how you are perceived. Choose a topic you feel passionate about. Be creative!

On-Campus and Alumni Interviews Matter

Interviews are the only personal interaction in an otherwise paper-driven process. Admissions committees frequently consider whether you bothered to set this up and what the interviewer thought of you. Aggressively seek out any official or unoffocial representatives of your Target List schools. You never know which contact you make will be the one that will move your application from the *Rejected* to the *Maybe* to the *Accepted* category.

Take Advantage of Family Ties

If you have siblings, parents, uncles, aunts, or grandparents who attended a school on your Target List, give that institution careful consideration because you have an edge there. Schools generally look favorably on relatives of students and alumni for obvious reasons—financial support, spirit, tradition, and so forth—and this may give you a leg up over nonaffiliated student-athletes who apply. Also, make sure to inform coaches if your father, mother, or any of your siblings have competed at the college level.

Get Recommendations

Since most college coaches on your Target List are not going to see you play in person, they will have to rely on recommendations from people they trust. It is extremely important to develop a network of credible and influential people who will provide recommendations. We recommend you ask the following people to write or call the college coaches on your Target List:

- High school coach
- Opposing high school coaches

- Any college coach or elite athlete in your sport
- Academy directors
- Influential alumni
- Camp directors and organizers
- Teammates who have gone on to compete in college

This is no time to be shy! Many adults are happy, if not flattered, to be asked to advocate for a young person who has taken the time to respectfully request their assistance. So ask. As we are sure you have heard many times before, the worst thing they can say is no.

Going on Campus Visits

Start Early

While campus visits are primarily junior- and senior-year events, there's no need to wait. Start visiting colleges as early as ninth grade. Take advantage of any chance to walk around a college campus. Check out schools in or near your hometown, stop by colleges during family trips, and visit older friends and siblings at school. The more visits you make, the better you will become at quickly sizing up a school and recognizing what you want from a college.

Unofficial Visits

Starting in your freshmen year of high school, you should take unofficial visits to a variety of schools. Even though you are responsible for paying all of the travel expenses, it's a great way to get a good read on a school so that you'll feel more confident when you develop your Target List a couple of years later. Make sure to let the coach know you are coming and that you want to stop by to introduce yourself. By making these visits regularly, you'll make a lasting and positive impression on the coaches whose help you may need come application time.

> **Chalk Talk**
>
> "The campus visit is absolutely essential. You need to spend a night or two and talk to students and professors. You need to see how you would fit in and how comfortable you would be there."
>
> —*Joe Hannah, Swimming Coach, LeMoyne College, NCAA D-II*

Official Visits

Coaches extend official visit invitations to their top recruits so that they can get to know the athletes better and promote their school's best features. Since official visits are an expense for the athletic program, only a limited number of athletes will receive these invitations. If you're fortunate enough to receive one in your junior or senior year, it's an outstanding opportunity for you to evaluate everything about the college and determine if the school and team fit your needs. Most of the time, you will stay with other athletes on the team and eat meals with them. This gives you an excellent opportunity to ask lots of questions. Keep in mind:

- The NCAA allows you one expenses-paid visit to five different schools. This restriction applies even if you are being recruited in two sports.
- Each visit may last a maximum of forty-eight hours.
- You must provide college authorities with your official transcript and entrance exam scores.
- You may return to one of the schools you've already visited, but you must pay all expenses.
- You must be registered with the NCAA Clearinghouse for official visits to NCAA schools.

Preplan Your Schedule

For unofficial visits, call the admissions office at least two weeks in advance to let them know you are coming to campus. An admissions counselor can tell you the dates and times for campus tours (they're usually held weekly), information sessions (a Q&A with an admissions office rep that takes place before the tour), and open houses (a day of events aimed at prospective students, scheduled once or twice a semester).

The counselor can also recommend classes to observe, help schedule individual meetings with faculty and coaches, and provide a campus map, a parking permit, and information on nearby lodging.

When to Go

The best time to visit is on a weekday in the fall or spring semester—not too close to the beginning of the semester and definitely not during finals week. That way, you'll see students and teachers going about their regular routines. For some families, however, a weekend, summer, or winter break visit may be easier to schedule.

While you obviously won't see an average day during those off times, you can still get a sense of the campus and the area. On a blitz tour of schools in a particular region, don't try to cram in more than two schools a day. It takes at least a half day to get an accurate feel for a campus, and, frankly, we think one school a day is a more appropriate pace.

Before Your Visit

Before your arrival, learn everything you can about the school. Read the school catalog and browse its website. Think of questions to ask that are not answered in published materials. (In other words, don't ask, "How many students go to school here?" Instead, ask questions such as "What percentage of freshmen drop out?" and "How do you help students in danger of failing?").

Decide beforehand what's important to you—anything from a strong political science department to single-sex dorms to a campus choir. Make a list of priorities and investigate them during your visit. Keep notes and try to ask the same questions at each school so that you have a means to compare them against each other.

What to Do on Campus

- Begin your visit with an information session and a campus tour.
- Sit in on a class.
- Check out the dorms.
- Eat in the cafeteria.
- Read the bulletin boards.
- Meet a faculty member and the coach.
- See the athletic facilities.
- Read the student newspaper.
- Try to find your favorite book on the library's computer system and then look for it in the stacks.

Remember to check out the area surrounding campus, too. What restaurants, stores, and recreation attractions are nearby? How close is the bus or train station? Think about what you'd need to live around there: A bike? A car? Warmer clothes?

If you visit with your parents, split up at some point so that you can roam the campus alone for a taste of what it would be like on your own in this new place. Parents can use this time to meet with a financial aid officer.

Also, make sure to check out the athletic facilities. Do they excite you? And by all means, watch the team practice or play a game, and see if you can visualize yourself as a member of this team.

Interviews

Some schools offer an interview with an admissions counselor as part of the campus visit. When you call the admissions office, ask if a personal interview is an option. If you have an interview, don't be nervous. The interview is mostly just a chance for you to ask questions of a school official and show that you are interested.

It's also an opportunity to make a positive impression on someone who may decide to go to bat for you in the application process, so make sure your prepared, respectful, and neat, and ask lots of questions.

Keep a Notebook Just for College Visits

Take notes while you're on campus, jotting down the name of the dorm you walked through, the class you visited, and the names of professors and students you met (and their phone numbers, so you can call back with follow-up questions). After each visit, write down your impressions—what you did and did not like about the school.

Take photos, especially if you visit during junior year, to help you remember each campus months later when you're deciding where to apply. Make sure to write thank-you notes to any school official who met with you individually.

Improper Recruiting Danger Signs

Most college coaches have your best interest at heart. However, you should be aware of improper recruiting tactics. Think twice if a coach does any of the following:

- Tells you that your scholarship commitment is four or five years. Even though most coaches will renew your scholarship each year, they can only promise it one year at a time.

- Guarantees you an easy academic schedule and shows little interest in you as a student
- Puts you in contact with a booster from the athletic department
- Speaks negatively about other colleges you're considering
- Offers you any monetary inducement, including college shirts or souvenirs. Be sure to speak with your high school coach if you are concerned about any awkward situation. Do not jeopardize your eligibility by ignoring an incident or sweeping it under the rug.

Sample Questions to Ask Athletes on the Team

- How do you like the coaches?
- Is it difficult keeping up with your schoolwork?
- How much time do you devote to the team in the off-season?
- What don't you like about the program?
- How accessible are the academic tutors?
- How are the living arrangements?
- If you could do it all over again, would you still choose this school?
- Do all the athletes hang out together?
- How many hours per day do you study?
- What do you do socially?
- How do the professors treat athletes?
- How do the other students on campus feel about athletes?

Sample Questions to Ask the Coach

- Are you interested in recruiting me, or will I have to walk on? (Avoid the temptation to ask the coach if he is going to offer you a scholarship. If the coach is interested in you, he will bring it up. It's similar to going to a job interview. Would your first question be "How much are you going to pay me?" Of course not!)
- What is the policy for walk-ons?
- What position do you see me playing?
- What is the off-season workout schedule?
- Will you redshirt me?
- If I suffer an injury or become academically ineligible, or you decide I'm just not good enough for the team, what happens to my scholarship, if I have one?

- What are the graduation rates for athletes on the team?
- Am I eligible for any other sources of financial aid?
- Are there academic tutors available?
- How many athletes are on the roster? Are their backgrounds similar to mine?
- Does the team take any special trips?
- Am I expected to arrive earlier than the beginning of the school year?
- Which coach will be working with me?
- Are there any team rules or policies I need to be aware of?
- What equipment does the team provide for the athletes?
- Will I have required study hall hours?
- How often does the team lift weights and condition?
- Is this a full-year commitment, or can I play other sports?

Questions to Ask Yourself after the Visit

- Did the coach have bad things to say about the other schools that are recruiting me?
- Would I attend this school if I had no intention of competing here?
- Do the coaches and athletes get along and respect one another?
- Will I be successful academically at this school? Athletically? How do I measure up to everyone else?
- Were the coaches and athletes I met honest, friendly, and interested in me, or did they seem to fake it?
- Did the coaches stress academics? Did they ask me about my educational and career goals? Were they knowledgeable about my area of study? If not, did they introduce me to someone to answer my questions?
- Did I respect the coach and his philosophy?
- Will I fit in at this particular school?
- Do I have what it takes to commit to this coach and team for four years?
- Does the school satisfy all requirements that I identified with my parents and counselor?

Hiring Recruiting Services

Why Recruiting Services May Not Be Effective

For a fee ranging from a couple hundred dollars to over $1,000, you can pay to have a recruiting service promote you to college coaches. They usually send a one-page profile and a highlight video to every school they believe is a good match. This could be several hundred schools or every school in the country.

The problem that coaches find with most recruiting services is that the person doing the evaluating is not credible, nor is it someone they personally know or respect. The evaluators tend to exaggerate your ability and project what level you can compete at by classifying you as a D-I, D-II, or D-III.

Categorizing athletes like this is flawed because the level of competition at each school varies so much within each division. In addition, the services bulk mail these profiles, so they are not personalized. This can be annoying for coaches.

Coaches believe that some of these services can be a waste of money and that they take advantage of athletes. It's your job to do comprehensive research. Understand that receiving questionnaires or camp invitations from coaches after using a recruiting service does not necessarily mean you are being recruited. Ask questions such as the following before you commit financially.

Sample Questions to Ask the Recruiting Service Before You Sign Up

- Who evaluates me, and does he have a financial interest in how he rates my skills? In other words, is he a salesman or a scout? (An unbiased evaluation has the most credibility with coaches.)
- Can you guarantee me a scholarship? (This is impossible to do.)
- Can anyone use this service, or do you have to possess the ability to compete in collegiate athletes? (The best services only accept athletes with college potential.)
- Can you provide the names and phone numbers of three athletes from my area who have used your service?
- What percentage of the athletes who use your service receive interest from college coaches?
- Have any coaches offered scholarships to athletes as a result of your service?
- Will you send my profile and video in its own envelope? (If it's sent with hundreds of others, it will not get the attention it deserves.)
- How many athletes receive no response even after all your promotion? (An honest service will tell you that most athletes do not receive interest from college coaches.)
- Do you offer a money-back guarantee?
- Which college coaches endorse your service?

What to Look for When Selecting a Recruiting Service

Choosing the right recruiting service to represent you to college coaches could mean the difference between continuing your athletic career or hanging up your uniform for good. Here are five criteria you should consider when choosing a company:

1. *Evaluators:* Who is grading your skills? It is extremely important that your evaluation is written by a knowledgeable and respected coach.

2. *Business history:* How long has the company been in business? Are they an unproven start-up, or have they been around for a while?

3. *Enrollment procedure:* Does the company represent any athlete who will pay its fee, regardless of ability? Make sure the service you choose limits enrollment to only athletes with college potential.

4. *References:* Are they willing to provide names of athletes' parents you can call who have used their service? If not, look elsewhere.

5. *Track record:* How many of their customers competed in college? Did any receive scholarships? Also, don't be impressed by their All-American alumnus who signs with a top college. Blue-chippers are going to receive attention regardless of the recruiting service.

Trying to Make the Team as a Walk-On

What Is a Walk-On?

Walk-on is a term used for an athlete who is not recruited but impresses the coaching staff during tryouts and is invited to join the team. Some teams are full of athletes who are not recruited. In fact many programs rely on walk-ons to keep their team competitive.

Four Types of Athletes Who Make Up a College Roster

1. Scholarship athletes

These athletes are the blue-chippers who are heavily recruited by many colleges and are expected to be major contributors immediately.

2. Athletes who are recruited but are not given athletic scholarship money

These athletes may also be heavily recruited but may not have the type of personal records to warrant athletic scholarship money. They usually receive many of the same benefits as the scholarship athletes, such as access to athletic housing, preregistration for classes, and in some cases guaranteed admittance to the school.

Some of these athletes may have even received scholarship offers at other schools but turned them down to attend more competitive academic institutions. These athletes are also expected to be contributors but not as quickly as a scholarship athletes.

3. Nonrecruited athletes who gain admittance to the school and let the coaching staff know that they would like to walk on

Athletes may have gone unnoticed in the recruiting process for various reasons. They may have been injured their senior years, they may be late bloomers, or their statistics are just not good enough for the coaches to think that they could contribute to the team. Fortunately, the recruiting process is not an exact science.

There are many All-American certificates given to athletes whom coaches didn't think were good enough to be recruited. Many walk-ons continue to develop through their college years while many recruited athletes never improve on their high school performances.

If you intend to walk on to a team, your best chance for success is to let the coach know of your intentions as soon as you gain admittance to the school. By doing this, the coach is able to follow your progress through your senior year.

The coach may even be able to give you workouts that you can do over the summer to prepare yourself for the fall training schedule. In some cases, athletic housing spots may open up so that you can room with another athlete. By notifying the coach of your intentions before school begins, you are showing a commitment to the sport, which any coach should respect. Even if a coach discourages you from walking on, be persistent and show your commitment.

Coaches receive many calls throughout the year from athletes who intend to walk on yet never show up. These coaches may just be trying to weed out athletes who are not committed to succeeding at the college level. While many walk-ons do not make it through four years of college, the ones who show the greatest desire and work ethic have the best chance to find themselves contributing to the team.

4. **Athletes who show up on the first day of school and ask to walk on**

These athletes rarely make the team. By failing to notify the coach ahead of time, they do not show signs of being committed to the sport. In many cases, practice may have already been going for a week, and at certain schools some teams have attended a preseason camp.

Attending Showcases

Showcases are usually one- or two-day events that attract about a hundred or more players who all desire to play college sports. Coaches and pro scouts from the region are invited to attend the workouts and evaluate each player's skills.

Most coaches are not allowed to communicate with players or parents at the event, and they usually stand off to the side to watch. Usually, all of the coaches watch one player perform a task at a time. This makes showcases outstanding opportunities for exposure.

While every player's ultimate goal is an athletic scholarship, keep in mind that a showcase is only one step in a long recruiting process. Very rarely will a coach make an offer to a player after seeing him at one event. The best time to start attending showcases is during your sophomore or junior year of high school.

This gives coaches a chance to follow your progress through high school, if you impressed them, and it gives you valuable experience in a tryout environment.

Chalk Talk

"I get about 150 letters each year, and I can't go through them all. I like to see each player compete myself. In that respect, the showcases are great because they help to cut through a lot of the fat. Occasionally, we do miss top players. However, in this day and age, with all those showcases, you would have to be at the North Pole for us not to find you."

—*Jeff Albies, Head Baseball Coach, William Patterson University, NCAA D-III*

College Coaches Like to Recruit at Showcases Because They Can . . .

- Evaluate many athletes in a short amount of time, especially those that have shown a genuine interest in attending their school
- Save money—showcases are cost-effective and allow coaches to consolidate their recruiting trips

You Should Attend Showcases Because You Can . . .

- Be seen in action by many coaches at one time

- Evaluate how your ability compares to others from your region

- Get an unbiased and professional opinion of your ability. After the show-case, make sure to ask the director for your scores.

- Determine your recruitability. You will know you made an impression if you receive letters or phone calls a few weeks later from coaches who attended the showcase.

- Receive experience competing in a pressure-filled environment. The more showcases you attend, the calmer and more relaxed you will be when they really count (during the summer and fall of your senior year).

Questions to Ask the Showcase Director before Registering

- Which coaches have committed to attend? (The biggest problem with show-cases is that it's hard to predict exactly which coaches will show up since they are not paid to be there.)

- Which coaches have attended the event during the last two years?

- How many athletes will attend the showcase?

- What is the format?

- How many athletes in the past have received interest or scholarships from coaches as a result of attending the showcase?

- Are there games? If yes, how much playing time can I expect?

- Do you provide references? (If he does, make sure to call them!)

- Is there a refund in case of bad weather?

- Will I receive college or pro instruction at the event?

Follow Up with Coaches

You may want to e-mail the coaches who attended the showcase and ask for their advice regarding what areas of your game need improvement and what kind of schools might need an athlete of your ability. Most coaches, regardless of their recruiting interest in you, will have notes from the showcase rating your ability. You never know who can help you. The more people you ask, the more opportunities you will have. Be aggressive!

What Not to Expect

College coaches will probably not do any of the following at a showcase:

- Announce themselves. Most coaches like to remain anonymous to prevent awkward conversations with athletes and parents.
- Offer you a scholarship at the event. The showcase is only one step in a long evaluation process.
- Expect you to perform perfectly. In fact, they want to see how you react after you make a mistake. Coaches are there to evaluate your skills and project what level they believe you could play at in two or three years.
- Treat you any differently because of your past accomplishments. Everyone gets the same opportunity to shine.
- Talk to you or your parents. If coaches are interested in you, they will follow up with a phone call or letter.

Tips for Making the Most of Your Showcase Experience

INFORM COACHES THAT YOU ARE ATTENDING THE SHOWCASE Write or e-mail coaches on your Target List, as well as coaches expected to attend, and tell them you will be participating in the showcase. Even if some of the schools on your list are located far away, the coaches may want to inform their local scouts to stop by and check you out.

DRESS IN A FULL UNIFORM It is important that you look like an athlete. Make sure to wear a jersey with your name on the back so that it is easy for a coach to identify you from the one hundred or so other athletes attending. First impressions are crucial, so wear a clean uniform, tuck your jersey in, and leave the jewelry at home.

HUSTLE Run at all times, even if others walk. You never know who is watching.

GET EVALUATED AT MULTIPLE POSITIONS Ask to be evaluated at every position that you play well. This will give coaches a chance to see more of you during the day. Also, you may be set on one primary position, but a coach may see more potential for you somewhere else. You are a more attractive recruit if you are versatile enough to play a variety of positions.

SPEND EVERY MINUTE OF DOWNTIME WISELY Since only one person is usually evaluated at a time, you will spend a lot of time on the sidelines waiting for your turn. If coaches are interested in you, they may want to keep an eye on you during these times. Don't fool around on the sidelines with your friends.

Instead, if it is allowed, use the downtime to practice. You will give interested coaches another opportunity to scout you. When you're on the field or court, never sit with your butt on the ground. Always take a knee, and hustle at all times.

Act like a ballplayer from the minute you alight from your car in the parking lot. There are coaches, recruiters, and scouts who will observe players arriving to get an idea of their attitudes. They will observe the player's dress—shirt tucked in neatly, hat not on backwards, and so on—and they will also make negative notes if the player has his parents run errands for him or acts disrespectful. Carry your own equipment—don't have your parents do it.

CHEERLEAD If others make great plays or need some encouragement, it's okay to cheer them on. Coaches will be impressed by your team spirit and leadership ability. A great way to be seen as a leader is to encourage teammates after they make a mistake, instead of berating them or criticizing them. Coaches are very aware of these kinds of players—the ones that pick each other up—and they are given bonus points.

ATTITUDE Attitude is extremely important! It's not so much how an athlete handles him- or herself during success but how they react to failure. If you make a mistake or error, don't slam your equipment or exhibit negative body language; instead, go onto the next play in a composed manner. The coach knows you made a mistake and wants to see how you handle it emotionally and mentally.

Also, your actual results during a showcase or tryout aren't as important as you might think. Most recruiters are observing your skills and not so much what you did. They're trying to project where you might be in a couple of years or so. If you show the right mechanics and have quick times in drills, that's more important than if you scored a goal or hit a home run or scored twenty points.

They'll be comparing your skills to the level of players you'll compete against in college, not so much what you did that day as far as results. A seven-footer at a basketball showcase, who's the tallest kid there, might score at ease, but the coach will watch his footwork, for instance, and estimate how he would have done against other players his height.

GET DIRTY Coaches love to recruit athletes who are not afraid to be extra aggressive. Just be sure that your hustle isn't "fake hustle" or "alibi hustle." A shortstop who throws his body to the ground after a grounder that is fifteen feet away and clearly out of his reach is showing the wrong kind of hustle, and a coach will spot that easily.

IF NO COACH SHOWS INTEREST IN YOU Do not assume that just because none of the attending coaches expressed interest in you after the showcase that you cannot compete on the college level. Keep the following in mind:

- Most coaches attend showcases with specific recruiting needs in mind. The coaches in attendance might not have a need for a athlete at your position.

- Coaches may be extremely impressed with your ability but may notice your GPA and test scores are too low. In this case, they cross you off their lists, no matter how good you are.
- The coaches who attend the showcase represent only a small sample of college teams. Remember, there are thousands of teams in the United States.
- There are lots of other showcases to attend. The more coaches that see you play, the better chance you will have of generating interest.

Producing a Highlight Video

A highlight video allows coaches who do not get an opportunity to see you in person evaluate your skills accurately. By watching your tape, coaches can assess your abilities personally and decide if you're a prospective recruit. They don't have to rely on someone else's evaluation, which may be biased.

Hold Up

When you are at a showcase, your every move is being evaluated. Here are some things that you should avoid:

- Arriving late
- Acting like you're a star or big man on campus
- Wearing a baseball cap backward
- Asking your parent to carry your bags or get you water
- Wearing earrings, bracelets, a watch, or a ponytail
- Getting upset if you don't perform well
- Asking the showcase evaluators your times and rankings before the event is over
- Not listening to where you're supposed to be
- Complaining or speaking negatively within earshot of anyone you don't know

---

Real Stories: The Showcase Showdown

Joshua Lyons, Ft. Lauderdale, FL

It's not necessarily who you know but rather who knows you that's important. This is the mentality I took when deciding to showcase my talent for college coaches and recruiters. True, my .417 BA and 14 HR during my junior year of high school spoke for themselves, but I needed to do more. I knew what my potential was, and now it was time for college coaches to find out for themselves. Attending a few showcases was the answer.

I suited up for two showcases here in Florida and made the trip to North Carolina for another—we take family vacations there every year, so it worked out nicely.

I was pretty nervous for the two local showcases, but I calmed down and played really well up north. However, in Florida, I got the chance to see how I compared to other kids from my area. Plus, with many top coaches and scouts in attendance, I got great exposure.

When I got back from North Carolina, there were letters and phone messages waiting from coaches who saw me play in Florida. It was nice to have coaches show interest in me rather than the other way around.

Eventually, I accepted an offer from a coach who saw me play here in Florida. He knew I was going to North Carolina and had another coach follow me there. He was impressed with my effort when he first saw me and wanted another opinion. I didn't even know he was sending someone to scout me. I guess you never know who is watching.

At a recent University of Tennessee baseball camp, a parent asked head coach Rod Delmonico what kind of importance he places on player highlight videos. He explained how helpful they are when judging the athlete's on-field ability but warned against producing amateur-looking footage.

While it isn't always necessary to hire a professional production company, the tape should have a professional feel to it. Parents should not be overheard cheering in the background, and the camera should remain steady and in focus. Little distractions like these could strip the video, and the athlete, of all credibility.

Coaches are not critiquing your video-editing skills, so don't worry about making yours look like a segment on ESPN. If you are concerned about producing your own video, you can hire professionals, who will do everything for you. If you choose to save the money (some company's will charge you $500 or more!) and do it yourself, follow these steps:

1. Use a combination of practice and game footage.
2. Wear a full uniform so you look like an athlete.
3. Get right to the action! Edit out all dead time, where there is no action.
4. Limit the length of the tape to four minutes. Coaches will not watch long videos. Less is better.
5. Use a tripod at all times so the camera doesn't shake.
6. Tell the cameraman or anyone within earshot to avoid "cheerleading." The only sound should come from the action on the field.
7. Make sure to shoot from angles that coaches want to see.
8. If you have access to video-editing software, you can shoot all the footage and edit it at home on your computer. If you don't, you will need to record over clips you do not want to include. The tape should only feature your best performances.
9. Convert the finished tape to VHS format and make as many copies as you need. Use a sticker to label the tape with your name, graduation year, position, address, and phone number. Make sure to write the title—for example, "Jeff Wilson's four-minute highlight tape ('05 grad)."

Introduction

Place the camera on a tripod a few feet away and introduce yourself. Speak clearly and confidently. Practice so it sounds conversational and not like you're reading a cue card. Include the following:

- Full name and graduation year
- High school's name and your coach's name
- City and state where you live
- Height and weight
- Positions
- SAT/ACT scores and GPA
- Rank in class
- What you want to study in college (if you're undecided, it's okay to say you're undecided, but just mention some of your interests at this point, such as liberal arts or business)

Finish Line

This was a long and information-packed chapter and one that you'll no doubt want to refer back to on many occasions.

Now that you have all this information about how to take an active role in your recruitment, it's time to get started. Here's a quick checklist of things you can begin doing:

- Prepare your written profile.
- Send out letters of interest to the schools on your Target List.
- Develop a webpage for yourself.
- Plan and take campus visits.

Travel, All-Star, and Select Teams

Research needs to be done to determine, first, which travel, all-star, and select teams to try out for to gain the maximum quality of experience and exposure, and, second, which college camps and showcase camps are truly valuable to attract the right college coaches' attention.

There are many "all-star," "traveling," and "select" teams, for instance, but many of these teams don't attract coaches to their games. The same holds true for showcase camps. Some of

Hold Up
Make sure you put all of your contact information—your full name, positions, address, and phone number—on a sticker on the outside of your videotape (both on top and on the spine). It's very possible that this tape might get separated from the rest of your materials in a college coach's office, and you don't want the coach to get you mixed up with another recruit. Remember, the easier you make it for the coaches, the more open they will be to you.

these camps may be expensive but don't really provide an effective showcase for the athlete. It's imperative to do your research before you invest your time and money.

All teams are not created equal. In recent years, their numbers have grown enormously, diluting the talent base. Just about anyone can create such a team.

It pays to do some research to determine if a particular team is truly made up of above-average players and if they compete against the kind of competition that a college coach views as superior.

One test to see if the team you're considering is a true select team is to gauge the competition they play against. If it's mostly local and their schedule is fairly indiscriminate, chances are they're not a bona fide select team. Some parents may pick teams that are "select" in their eyes only.

Also, just because a team "travels" does not mean that the team is an elite one, composed of superior players. A true select team comprises high-caliber players and plays the level of competition that regularly attracts college and pro coaches and scouts to their contests.

If college coaches don't normally attend at least a few of the games to see the players on that team, it may not be the best team to get noticed on. It doesn't really count if the coach of such a team claims that there have been scouts at their games if the only reason is that the college coaches and scouts were there because they were scouting the opposing team.

That would be relying on lightning to strike, and the odds aren't in your favor if you hope to get noticed by accident on such a team.

What Is Their Focus?

Is it primarily to prepare players (the younger-aged teams) for high school ball? If so, that might not give you the exposure you're looking for. A true select team very likely takes the assumption, based on the quality of players selected, that your high school tryout will most likely be the easiest tryout you'll have.

A true select team should focus on your development as a college or pro player. Teams that truly have that kind of focus are ordinarily the teams that college coaches are interested in watching, as they know the talent level on the team is more likely going to be what they're after.

How Many Games Do They Play?

If they play relatively few games, especially in a cold climate, then they probably aren't a bona fide select team. If you're a baseball player in Indiana, for instance, and the team you're considering only plays forty to fifty games in a season, that's probably not a true select team. You'll play more than that in a rec league but not nearly enough to gain the kind of playing experience that a player from, say, Florida or Texas will have, who will play at least twice as many games.

Who Do They Play?

Is their competition high-level competition, or are you aware of other teams that play much tougher teams regularly?

Who Coaches the Team?

Is it the father of one of the players? Many of the best select teams don't allow parents to coach their own offspring (for obvious reasons). Also, is the coach paid, or does he or she work on a volunteer basis? Many of the best select teams pay their coaches. Also, what are the coach's qualifications? Did he or she play college or professional ball?

What's the Team Practice-to-Games Ratio?

If it's all games and only a few or no practices, it may still be a good-quality team, but many times teams that don't practice much don't really teach the players much either. At higher ages, practices may be fewer, as most players will also participate on the high school level during that season, and the summer teams take that into consideration. At younger levels, however, the practice-to-games ratio is more important.

How Many Players Make the Team?

If the number is so large that it's obvious that several players aren't going to get much playing time, then that team might not be a good fit. A baseball or softball team carrying, say, sixteen players means that at least three or four will probably log a lot of pine time. A basketball team with fourteen players would probably result in the same situation.

The same applies for most sports—if they carry an inordinate amount of players, consider how much actual playing time you'll receive. It's more important to play a lot for a lesser team than to sit on the bench for a more prestigious team.

What If I Can't Make a Select or Travel Team or Can't Afford One?

Don't worry about it! It does help for most players simply because as a rule you'll compete against better competition, have better coaching, and get much more experience, but sometimes it's just not practical or possible to be on such a team.

If, for any reason, you can't get on a select team, then make up for it in other ways—practice more individually, get private coaching, and so on.

Drive Down the Cost of College

In this chapter:

- [ ] NCAA scholarships by sport for D-I and D-II programs
- [ ] Where to find scholarship money other than for athletics
- [ ] How to determine how much money you need and how much your family contribution will be
- [ ] The various types of financial aid and when forms should be submitted
- [ ] Tips for receiving a good aid package and where to find loans

This chapter may have you scratching your head. After all, if a goal of this guide is to help you get an athletic scholarship, why do you need to worry about paying for college? Well, as we've said before, athletic scholarships are difficult to obtain, and most don't cover all of your costs. Even if you're the next superstar, the chances are good you're going to have to pay for at least some of your college expenses and possibly locate any scholarship or financial aid dollars to assist you and your parents with the upcoming costs.

NCAA Scholarships by Sport

The following table lists the allowable number of scholarships for NCAA Divisions I and II. This does not suggest that each college program offers the full amount of possible scholarships for each sport. That decision is governed by each school's sports budget and other factors.

NCAA DIVISION I		
Sport	Men's	Women's
Baseball	11.7	12
Softball		
Basketball	13	15
Track and Field	12.6	18
Football	85	0
Golf	4.5	6
Gymnastics	6.3	12
Field Hockey	0	12
Ice Hockey	18	18
Lacrosse	12.6	12
Swimming Diving	9.9	8.1
Tennis	4.5	8
Volleyball	4.5	12
Water Polo	4.5	8
Wrestling	9.9	0

NCAA DIVISION II		
Sport	Men's	Women's
Baseball	9	7.2
Softball		
Badminton	0	10
Basketball	10	10
Bowling	0	5
Track and Field	12.69	12.69
Fencing	4.5	4.5
Football	36	0
Golf	3.6	5.4
Gymnastics	5.4	6
Handball	0	12
Field Hockey	0	6.3
Ice Hockey	13.5	18
Lacrosse	10.8	9.9
Rifle	3.6	7.2
Rowing	0	20
Skiing	6.3	6.3
Squash	9	7.2
Swimming Diving	0	9
Synchronized Swimming	0	5
Tennis	4.5	6
Volleyball	4.5	8
Water Polo	4.5	8
Wrestling	9	0

Facts about Financial Aid

Athletic Scholarships

Once again, we remind you that being realistic about the financial aspect of college is just as important as setting your admission and athletic expectations. Next to purchasing a home, paying for college is the biggest investment you or your parents will likely face. Everyone in the family needs to be on the same page when anticipating expenses and how to reduce them.

> **Catch This**
>
> If you would like to compare the costs of your target schools, use our worksheet Cost of College Comparison, in chapter 8 (p. 135).

Financial Aid Helps Roughly 75 Percent of All Students Afford College

Simply put, as much as athletic and academic concerns should dictate your Target List schools, the price of college may ultimately have even more to do with where you receive your higher education. Because the cost of college is high and probably rising—tuition for four years averages $99,784 at a private college or $45,352 at a public university—you should definitely consider applying for financial aid to help pay your college expenses.

Overall college costs can, and should be, an important consideration in your final selection process. With a little research and dedication, however, you can avoid having the expense of college dictate which schools you apply to and attend. Here are many ways to alleviate the financial burden, and you must employ a creative plan and investigate all areas of help.

Become familiar with all the sources of aid that are available to you, and constantly stay abreast of this ever-changing landscape. This chapter includes tips on scholarships and financial aid, but we urge you to speak with your guidance counselor and to research websites such as www.wiredscholar.com, www.collegeboard.com, www.scholarships.com, and www.fastweb.com.

Over Six Hundred Thousand Scholarship Opportunities Available!

Www.fastweb.com, an Internet scholarship search site, features information on over six hundred thousand different scholarships and aid programs. Even though it takes a lot of time and paperwork to win this "free" money, it could save your family a lot of money. That makes it well worth the effort. We've already explained how tough it is to get an athletic scholarship, and when you consider that NCAA D-I Ivy and Patriot League schools (other than American University, recently admitted to the Patriot League), all NCAA D-III schools, and all NJCAA D-III schools do not even offer athletic scholarships, you'll understand how important it can be to locate other aid.

Determine How Much Money You Need

Get out the notebook and calculator. The following is a list of general-expense categories, which are part of any college student's budget. To give you and your parents a general idea of how much money it will take to get you through college and launched into adulthood, do some research to come up with approximate figures for each of these categories. Add it all up, and you've got yourself a budget, which needs to be funded from one or more of the following: your parents, your working wages, your savings, and any scholarships or aid programs available to you.

Budget Categories for Your College Education

- Tuition and fees
- Room and board
- Books and classroom supplies
- Personal expenses
- Transportation

A number of sites, such as the ones mentioned here, have a variety of guides and calculators that let you plug in schools and numbers to come up with anticipated costs for your education.

Family Contribution

Most colleges will expect you and your parents to contribute to your college expenses based on your parent's annual income and their assets. When referring to the Estimated Family Contribution schedule (see chapter 8, p. 136), you will need to know your parents' net assets and annual income before taxes.

Take the net assets and read down according to your family size until you get to your parent's annual income, and this will determine your family contribution. Subtract your family contribution from the college cost, and the result will indicate the amount of aid that can be available.

Example: If your parents' net assets are $40,000 and their annual income is $44,000 for a family of three, then your family contribution will be $6,869. If the college cost is $15,000, then your aid eligibility would be $8,131.

Loans, Grants, Merit Scholarships, and Work-Study

So where does the money come from to send you to school? It can come in the form of loans, grants, scholarships, and federal work-study grants. Need-based loans are granted through Perkins or Stafford Loan programs. The federal government may also distribute loans to families who have trouble meeting their family contribution. Congress has two programs to assist families in this situation; they are the Parent Loans for Undergraduate Students (PLUS) and the Supplemental Loans for Students (SLS). More than 60 percent of all financial aid comes in the form of student loans.

Many need-based financial aid packages may include grants or scholarships. In addition, the college you attend may reward you with a special grant or scholarship for distinguished achievements within a particular area, such as academics or athletics.

> **Hold Up**
>
> You should be careful that your on-campus job is not so time-consuming that it detracts from your studies. Also, be aware that if you play a sport, your athletic obligation will require a considerable amount of your free time.

The federal work-study program is designed to provide students with on-campus jobs. The jobs range from giving campus tours to filing books in the library. The money you earn in work-study is paid directly to you on a weekly or monthly basis, depending on the school. It can be used to help pay tuition, room and board, books, or any personal expenses.

Financial Aid Forms

To apply for financial aid, you and your parents will have to complete the Free Application for Federal Student Aid (FAFSA). The form can be downloaded from www.fafsa.ed.gov, or you can get it from you local high school guidance counselor. It compiles all your family's finances and rates the information to determine your eligibility for aid. Other forms may include the FAF (Financial Aid Form), the SAAC (Student Aid Application for California), and the FFS (Family Financial Statement).

College Scholarship Service/Financial Aid PROFILE

Some colleges that offer institutional financial aid ask applicants to complete a "profile" in addition to the FAFSA. The profile requests much more comprehensive and detailed financial information. If asked to submit this form, you should do it because it could lead to additional money. Call 800-778-6888 to register, and an application packet will be mailed to you. The application costs $6 to process and $16 for each report they send to schools and organizations.

Timeline

Financial aid forms should be completed and submitted no later than February of your senior year so that you are eligible for assistance. By mid-April, you will receive an award letter from each school where you have been accepted. The packages will vary at each school and may include federal and state grants, school scholarships, student loans, and on-campus jobs. This will allow you to determine which school is offering you the best package.

The Relationship between the Financial Aid and Admissions Offices

Most schools claim that their admissions office and financial aid office are independent and do not influence each other's decisions. Usually, the best overall students are admitted regardless of their financial need, and the average students are evaluated based on how much money they will cost the school.

Tips for Receiving the Best Package

Apply to Expensive Schools, Even If You Need a Lot of Aid

If an expensive college sees you as a desirable candidate, you should definitely apply, regardless of your financial situation. As long as you have a financial need, the school will provide the money you need. Believe it or not, you could actually pay less to attend a high-tuition private school than a lower-cost state school. Knowing that your family contribution can be roughly the same at schools with varying costs will enable you to concentrate on nonfinancial considerations in selecting schools to apply to.

If your parents' income is too high and you do not qualify for need-based aid, you may find that merit aid puts a high-sticker school within reach. Colleges are awarding more merit aid packages to attract higher-caliber students. Most colleges are able to meet the financial needs of all of their students, but keep in mind that a lot of packages feature mostly federal loans and work-study and fewer grants. And that means you will be paying off these loans for years to come.

Negotiate a Better Deal at Your First-Choice School by Playing Colleges against Each Other

Most aid administrators agree that if you don't get the aid you think you need, you should appeal your case. Your circumstances may warrant a second look, or a mistake on your applications could come to light. Frequent mistakes include claiming college expenses for a sibling who has dropped out and stating your adjusted gross income instead of the total.

If you want to try to increase your financial aid package, make sure you do it in a tactful way. Ask the financial aid officer if you can "appeal" your offer. Don't use the term "negotiate," because it has a negative connotation. Explain that you really want to go to the school and you would really appreciate it if the school would consider adjusting your package.

Be honest and provide copies of the other offers you have received. Explain how much of an increase you need before you can enroll. You have nothing to lose by asking. Even though most financial aid officers do not want to get dragged into a bidding war, you should still request a better package with your first-choice school. If you're a highly sought-after prospect, the school will make every effort to meet your request.

Ask your guidance counselor to call the financial aid department and request the adjustment on your behalf. Most students who take this route find that their package increases. Also, if you win an outside scholarship, make sure to get the scholarship provider involved. Big companies who provide scholarships have a lot of clout with financial aid officers. If a school upsets a parent or student with its policy, it's just one student and one tuition at stake. But the school risks a wealth of future funding when they displease a prominent scholarship provider.

Watch Out for Scam Artists!

Watch out for "financial aid advisors" who offer their services for a fee and do any of the following things:

- Promise you a scholarship. (No one can guarantee you an award.)
- Say the scholarships they will help you find are not publicized. (Scholarships widely publicize their competitions because they want to choose the winner from a throng of applicants.)
- Offer to search a scholarship database for you. (Never pay for this service— it's free!)
- Pressure you to commit right away. (Avoid fast-talking salesmen.)
- Ask inappropriate questions about your finances or related information. (It is none of their business.)
- Request your bank or credit card account number to "hold" a scholarship for you. (Never provide this information.)
- Invite you to a free financial planning "seminar." When families arrive, they're hit with a high-pressure sales pitch for costly services that may include career counseling, rearranging assets to increase a family's calculated need for aid, and an "exclusive" scholarship search that, in reality, you could perform at little or no cost. (The services can run as much as $1,000 and offer little or nothing of worth—sometimes a basic skills assessment, perhaps, or canned financial advice.)

Tips for Getting the Most Aid

- Alert the aid office before you apply to irregularities regarding your parents' finances, such as an upcoming one-time bonus, pending hospital bills, an inheritance, a business start-up, or serious reversal of fortune. The more the office knows, the better.
- Beat the deadline and submit your application before it is due. Dealing with a family's tangled finances during crunch time puts tremendous pressure on

overworked aid representatives. That's when mistakes happen. Also, a lot of aid is awarded on a first-come, first-served basis.

- Get organized. Keep your files updated, know the facts, and maintain a call log to verify whom you've been talking with, when you talked to them, and the content of those conversations.

- Go to the top. If you're not satisfied with what you're hearing from an aid representative, ask politely but firmly to speak with the director of financial aid. Most directors say their phone lines are open to anyone who calls.

- Always answer financial aid applications honestly. If an aid officer ever notices a discrepancy between what you write on your application and your parents' tax returns, you will need to repay the money owed, plus fines.

Legitimate Ways to Help Increase Your Aid Package

- Use savings to pay off credit cards, car loans, or other debt. These items are not figured into your family's net assets. The lower your family's assets and income, the more aid you will receive.

- Avoid taking large capital gains in the year used to determine aid. These gains count as both assets and income.

- Reduce assets in the student's name. Federal law requires that 35 percent of those assets must be defined as the student's share of first-year expenses, while the take is no more than about 5.6 percent of parents' assets (and roughly $40,000 is not counted).

- Notify the financial aid office in writing about anything unusual in your family's financial situation, such as a large medical expense.

Apply for Local Scholarships

Many corporations and nonprofit organizations offer scholarship competitions. Your high school's guidance office probably keeps a list of scholarships, and it's smart to call organizations to see if they offer awards. Churches and synagogues, as well as 4-H, Rotary, Kiwanis, Lions, and Boys & Girls clubs are all good places to start. The Internet site www.fastweb.com is also a great resource. Some of these scholarships may only amount to a few hundred dollars, but every little bit helps!

Write the Best Application Essays You Can

It will be well worth the effort. Ask your parents and teachers to critique your drafts. You can reuse the same essay for different applications, but make sure to personalize it for the specific award.

Low-Interest Rates on College Loans Available

If your family is like most others in the United States and is unable to completely afford college expenses, you can take out a low-interest loan. (The rates have fallen at the time of publication to their lowest levels in years.) Remember, you don't need to borrow the amount needed for all four years. You just need enough to get you through one year at a time.

Tuition Payment Plans

For roughly $50 per year, Academic Management Services (508-235-2900), a financial service company can spread your tuition payments over ten to twelve months, interest-free. This way you don't have to pay the entire first-year bill in one lump sum. Many universities also offer an interest-free monthly payment plan, managed either by a company like Academic Management Services or by the school itself.

Free Aid Information Available Online

Two of the best websites, say financial aid experts, are FastWeb (www.fastweb.com) and *U.S. News & World Reports* (www.usnews.com). Both feature comprehensive searchable databases of scholarships into which you can enter information such as age, gender, class rank, and track of study and pull up a list of grants and loans that fit your profile.

Be Careful about How Much Money You Borrow

Last year, more than five million students borrowed a record $40 billion for college, three times the 1990 level. At some schools, graduates leave campus with an average debt of $30,000. To make matters worse, most undergraduates misjudge how much they're going to owe after they leave college and how this debt might affect their future plans.

To avoid any surprises, visit an aid officer periodically during college, beginning in January of your freshman year; keep track of how fast the loans are piling up; and get some help on how to build your loan repayment obligations into compensation you will receive when you enter the workforce.

One way to stay abreast of your accumulating federal debt is by visiting the National Student Loan Data System (www.nslds.ed.gov), which provides personalized information online.

Finish Line

Sadly, there are a lot of families who mistakenly believe that their child's tuition will be fully paid for when they receive an athletic scholarship. Too often, these families get a rude awakening when their children do not get a full ride or no scholarship at all.

Now's the time to take an honest look at your family's financial situation and begin to look at your options for paying for college. Here are some steps to follow:

- Use FastWeb or another service to identify some scholarships you might qualify for.
- Contact local companies and organizations and your school's guidance department to identify local scholarship opportunities.
- Apply for as many scholarships as you can.
- Look into loans and other means of getting aid.
- Work on your application essays.

The College Landscape by Division

In this chapter:

☐ NCAA Division I   ☐ NJCAA D-I

☐ NCAA Division II   ☐ NJCAA D-II

☐ NCAA Division III   ☐ NJCAA D-III

☐ NAIA

Now, it's time to get a clear picture of just how many options you truly have. This chapter details the eligibility requirements for each of the divisions.

National Collegiate Athletic Association (NCAA)

The NCAA is the most powerful governing body for college sports. It represents three divisions (I, II, and III) featuring 1,024 four-year schools.

NCAA Clearinghouse

You must register with the NCAA Clearinghouse after your junior year if you want to be considered an eligible recruit. This lets colleges know that you have met all their academic requirements.

Contact Info

NCAA

700 W. Washington St.

P.O. Box 6222

Indianapolis, IN 46206-6222

Web: www.ncaa.org

Phone: 317-917-6222

Fax: 317-917-6888

Publications: 888-388-9748

NCAA Clearinghouse

P.O. Box 4044

Iowa City, IA 52243-4044

Phone: 319-337-1492 or 888-388-9748

Fax: 319-337-1556

To check the status of your filing: 319-339-3003

To register, call 888-388-9748 to receive your free copy of the *NCAA Guide for the College-Bound Student-Athlete*. This guide provides detailed information about the NCAA's requirements and contains a student release form. Mail or fax the white copy of the form to the Clearinghouse with the $30 registration fee. Give the yellow and pink copies of the form to your guidance counselor, who will send the yellow copy along with your transcript to the Clearinghouse.

The Clearinghouse will send your eligibility status to any NCAA D-I or D-II school that requests it.

NCAA Division I

D-I schools mostly comprise big schools that attract considerable media attention. They have the largest athletic budgets and recruit athletes nationally. They are the most popular with high school students because of their high-profile status. There are 326 D-I schools in the country (117 I-A, 121 I-AA, 88 I-AAA).

Academic Eligibility Requirements—Division I

Depending on your three criteria—GPA, SAT/ACT exam scores, and core courses—you will either be classified as a *qualifier*, *partial qualifier*, or *nonqualifier*. Here are the requirements for each.

Qualifier Requirements

- Graduate high school
- Graduate with a core-course GPA (based on a 4.0 scale) and total SAT/ACT scores based on the qualifier index (see the following section)
- Successfully complete a core curriculum of at least thirteen academic course units:
  - Four years of English
  - Two years of math
  - Two years of social science
  - Two years of natural or physical science (including one lab class)
  - One additional year in English, math, or natural or physical science
  - Two more years of any of the above or foreign language, computer science, philosophy, or nondoctrinal religion

Qualifier Index

Core-Course GPA	ACT	SAT
3.550+	37	400
3.525	38	410
3.500	39	420
3.475	40	430
3.450	41	440
3.425	41	450
3.400	42	460
3.375	42	470
3.350	43	480
3.325	44	490
3.300	44	500
3.275	45	510
3.250	46	520
3.225	46	530

Core-Course GPA	ACT	SAT
3.200	47	540
3.175	47	550
3.150	48	560
3.125	49	570
3.100	49	580
3.075	50	590
3.050	50	600
3.025	51	610
3.000	52	620
2.975	52	630
2.950	53	640
2.925	53	650
2.900	54	660
2.875	55	670
2.850	56	680
2.825	56	690
2.800	57	700
2.775	58	710
2.750	59	720
2.725	59	730
2.700	50	730
2.675	61	740–750
2.650	62	760
2.625	63	770
2.600	64	780
2.575	65	790
2.550	66	800
2.525	67	810
2.500	68	820
2.475	69	830
2.450	70	840–850
2.425	70	860
2.400	71	860
2.375	72	870
2.350	73	880
2.325	74	890
2.300	75	900
2.275	76	910
2.250	77	920

Core-Course GPA	ACT	SAT
2.225	78	930
2.200	79	940
2.175	80	950
2.150	81	960
2.100	82	970
2.075	83	980
2.050	84	990
2.025	85	1000
2.000	86	1010

Partial Qualifier Requirements

- Graduate high school
- Graduate with a core-course GPA (based on a 4.0 scale) and total SAT/ACT scores based on the partial qualifier index (see following section)
- Successfully complete a core curriculum of at least thirteen academic course units (same courses as qualifier requirements)

If you are a partial qualifier, you cannot play in games during your first year at a Division I school, but you can practice with the team at the home facility and receive a scholarship. You will have three seasons left of eligibility. You can earn a fourth year of eligibility if you receive a bachelor's degree before the start of your fifth year of college.

Partial Qualifier Index

Core-Course GPA	ACT	SAT
2.75	59	720
2.725	59	730
2.700	60	730
2.675	61	740–750
2.650	62	760
2.625	63	770
2.600	64	780
2.575	65	790
2.550	66	800
2.525	67	810

Nonqualifier

You will be classified as a nonqualifier if you fail to graduate from high school or do not meet the core-curriculum GPA and SAT/ACT scores required for a qualifier.

If you are a nonqualifier, you cannot practice with the team, play games, or receive a scholarship during your first year. You will have three seasons left of eligibility. You can earn a fourth year of eligibility if you receive a bachelor degree before the start of your fifth year of college.

NCAA Division II

D-II schools are medium-sized schools and recruit on a smaller scale and have fewer scholarship opportunities than D-I schools. There are 279 D-II schools.

Academic Eligibility Requirements—Division II

Depending on your three criteria—GPA, SAT/ACT exam scores, and core course—you will either be classified as a *qualifier, partial qualifier,* or *nonqualifier.* Here are the requirements for each.

Qualifier Requirements

- Graduate high school
- Graduate with a 2.0 core-course GPA (based on a 4.0 scale)
- Score a combined SAT score of at least 820 or a 68 sum score on the ACT
- Successfully complete a core curriculum of at least thirteen academic course units as follows:
  - Three years of English
  - Two years of math
  - Two years of social science
  - Two years of natural or physical science (including one lab class)
  - Two additional years of English, math, or natural or physical science
  - Two more years of any of the above or foreign language, computer science, philosophy, or nondoctrinal religion

Partial Qualifier

- Graduate high school
- Score a combined SAT score on the verbal and math sections of 820 or a 68 sum score on the ACT, or . . .
- Graduate with a 2.0 core-course GPA (based on a 4.0 scale) and successfully complete a core curriculum of at least thirteen academic courses (same as qualifier requirements)

If you are a partial qualifier, you cannot play in games during your first year, but you can practice with the team at the home facility and receive a scholarship. You will have four seasons left of eligibility.

Nonqualifier Requirements

You will be classified as a nonqualifier if you fail to graduate from high school or do not meet the core-curriculum GPA and SAT/ACT scores required for a qualifier. If you are a nonqualifier, you cannot practice with the team, play games, or receive a scholarship during your first year. You will have four seasons left of eligibility.

NCAA Division III

D-III schools tend to recruit regionally, do not offer scholarships, but comprise some of the most prestigious academic schools in the country. There are 419 D-III schools, and none offer scholarships, though many offer generous academic scholarships.

Academic Eligibility Requirements—Division III

D-III schools do not have standard requirements. Check with the individual schools that interest you for details.

National Association of Intercollegiate Athletics (NAIA)

The NAIA represents 288 four-year schools. The National Association of Intercollegiate Athletics, an athletic league completely separate from the NCAA, began in 1937. The organization is divided into thirty-two districts representing

Contact Info

NAIA

23500 W. 105th St.

P.O. Box 1325

Olathe, KS 66051

Web: www.naia.org

Phone: 913-791-0044

the fifty states, and it sponsors district and national championships in a variety of sports. Similar to the NCAA, the NAIA awards full or partial scholarships, if students meet eligibility requirements.

Academic Eligibility Requirements

You must meet two of the following three eligibility requirements:

- Graduate in the upper half of your high school class
- Earn a combined score of at least 860 on the SAT or 68 on the ACT
- Earn a 2.0 cumulative GPA (based on a 4.0 scale)

For a complete list of eligibility requirements, procedures, guidelines, and association bylaws, call the NAIA and ask to receive a copy of their manual, *A Guide for the College-Bound Athlete.*

National Junior College Athletic Association (NJCAA)

The NJCAA consists of 503 two-year programs representing three divisions (I, II, and III). D-I and D-II schools offer up to twenty-four scholarships, depending on the sport. D-III schools do not offer scholarships.

The NJCAA has member schools in forty-two states and is the national governing body of fifteen men's and twelve women's sports over three divisions. Approximately 45,300 athletes compete in one of twenty-four regions, and every year the NJCAA hosts forty-eight national championships.

If you yearn for the experience of living in a dorm, spending Saturday afternoons cheering for the home football team, and enjoying an active social life, you should choose a four-year school. If not, a junior college may be a perfect option for you. While most JCs offer a wide array of extracurricular activities, the students commute and many of them work full-time, so they have less time for social activities.

You have two options if you attend a JC. The first is called a transfer program, which enables you to leave school after one or two years and transfer your credits earned to a four-year school. The second option is called a terminal program, which earns you an associate's degree after attending school for two years.

Academic Requirements

JCs generally offer an open-door admission policy so you don't have to worry about getting in. You must, however, meet one of the following requirements:

- Graduate from high school
- Receive a high school equivalency diploma
- Pass a national test, such as the General Education Development (GED) Test

Hold Up

Hold Up: Club Teams Offer Opportunities Too!

Don't forget to explore club sports opportunities at schools that interest you. Club teams exist in almost every school in the country, and some have just as much practice time and competition as varsity sports. In some cases, club teams eventually become varsity sports or become eligible to receive some funding from athletic departments.

Previous club teams that turned varsity include golf, volleyball, water polo, ultimate frisbee, and crew. Go to the athletic department and talk to the athletic director or someone on the staff to get things rolling. You have to advertise the sport with posters and announcements around the school to get participants and spectators; you may also have to find a coach. It might be an arduous process but one well worth it in the end.

For a complete list of eligibility requirements, procedures, guidelines, and association bylaws, call the NJCAA and ask to receive a copy of their manual, *NJCAA Handbook and Casebook*.

Letter of Intent

The NJCAA letter of intent is used to commit an individual to a specific institution for a period of one year and is only valid for NJCAA colleges. You may sign a letter of intent with both a NJCAA college and a NCAA college, but you may not sign a letter of intent with two NJCAA colleges. If you sign a letter of intent with two NJCAA colleges, you will be ineligible for one year.

Contact Info

NJCAA

1755 Telstar Dr.

Colorado Springs, CO 809920

Phone: 719-590-9788

Web: www.njcaa.org

Benefits of Attending a Junior College

Attending a two-year junior or community college is a great option for many athletes. Here are some reasons why you may want to consider the JC route.

YOUR GPA, SAT/ACT, OR CORE COURSES DID NOT MEET THE FOUR-YEAR SCHOOLS' REQUIREMENTS If you did not apply yourself academically in high school and your marks are not indicative of your full potential, you might be better off starting college with a year or two of JC and then transferring to a four-year school.

YOU NEED ANOTHER YEAR AT HOME BEFORE GOING AWAY TO SCHOOL If you think that another year living at home would help ease the transition to a four-year college, then a local JC is a good option.

YOU DON'T WANT TO COMPETE AT ANY OF THE FOUR-YEAR SCHOOLS TO WHICH YOU'VE BEEN ACCEPTED If you got a late start preparing for college and are not happy with the schools you've been admitted to, a year of JC exposure may give you a better opportunity to fully explore all your four-year options.

YOUR FAMILY CANNOT AFFORD TO SEND YOU TO A FOUR-YEAR SCHOOL AT THIS TIME Tuition at JCs is inexpensive, and athletic scholarships are more plentiful. Even if you don't receive a scholarship, you can attend most for only a couple of thousand dollars a year.

YOU ALSO WANT TO WORK FULL-TIME A JC is also a practical choice for students who need class schedules flexible enough to accommodate full-time jobs. The schools typically offer classes from 8 AM to 10 PM weekdays and on Saturday mornings to accommodate students with jobs.

Websites by Sport

Basketball

National Association of Basketball Coaches (www.nabc.org)

Women's Basketball Coaches Association (www.wbca.org)

www.Thebasketballportal.com: basketball-related links

www.Basketball-toplinks.com: all basketball-related links

www.collegehoopsnet.com: college news, basketball links, recruiting info

www.Rivalshoops.com: college basketball recruiting news and links

www.Hoopmasters.com: college basketball recruiting news

www.D3hoops.com: Division III news and info

Soccer

National Soccer Coaches Association of America (www.nscaa.com)

www.Soccer-corner.com: soccer-related links

www.Thesoccerportal.com: soccer-related links

www.Soccer-toplinks.com: soccer-related links

www.Soccerinfo.com: camps, tournaments, recruiting info

Hockey

American Hockey Coaches Association (www.ahcahockey.com)

American Women's Hockey Coaches Association
(www.brown.edu/Athletics/Womens_Hockey/AWHCA)

www.collegehockey.org: college, prep, junior, and pro news, links, camps

www.Azhockey.com: links, news, stats

www.Uscollegehockey.com: college stats, standings, news, polls

www.Hockeydb.com: Internet database, stats, leagues, message boards

www.Thehockeyportal.com: hockey-related links

Baseball

American Baseball Coaches Association (www.abca.org)

www.Baseball-links.com: baseball-related links

www.Hsbaseballweb.com: high school baseball news, links, showcases

www.Aaronslinks.com: baseball-related links

www.Heavyhitter.com: baseball-related links

www.Thebaseballportal.com: baseball-related links

Softball

National Fastpitch Coaches Association (www.nfca.org)

www.Softballsearch.eteamz.com: links, bulletin boards, tips, drills

www.Softballtournaments.com: tournament listing, links, forums

www.Playnsa.com: National Softball Association

www.Softball.org: Amateur Softball Association of America

Field Hockey

National Field Hockey Coaches Association (www.nfhca.org)

www.Usfieldhockey.com: official site of U.S.A. field hockey

www.Hockeylinx.com: hockey-related links

www.Planetfieldhockey.com: international news, coaching and training tips

Wrestling

National Wrestling Coaches Association (www.nwcaonline.com)

www.Ncwa.net: National Collegiate Wrestling Association

www.Themat.com: camps, links, news, rankings, results

www.Intermatwrestle.com: news, results, links, camps, forums

www.Amateurwrestler.com: forums, training and health tips

Tennis

United States High School Tennis Association (www.ushsta.org)

www.Thetennisportal.com: tennis-related links

www.collegetennisonline.com: news, rankings, links to camps

www.collegeandjuniortennis.com: news, rankings, schedules

www.Itatennis.com: Intercollegiate Tennis Association

www.Tennisserver.com: news, links, rules, organizations, tips

www.Tennis4all.com: links, info, message boards, organizations

Track/Cross Country

United States Track Coaches Association (www.ustrackcoaches.org)

United States Cross Country Coaches Association (www.usccca.org)

www.Dyestat.com: high school track portal

www.Track-and-field.net: links, stats, news, track merchandise

www.Tflinks.com: track-and-field links

www.Usatf.org: links, merchandise, rules

www.Trackinfo.org: links, events

Golf

National Golf Coaches Association (www.ngca.com/index.jsp)

www.Cgfgolf.org: College Golf Foundation

www.Nagce.org: National Association for Golf Coaches and Educators

Lacrosse

U.S. Lacrosse (www.lacrosse.org)

Intercollegiate Women's Lacrosse Coaches Association (www.iwlca.org)

www.Laxlinks.com: lacrosse-related links

www.Youthlacrosseusa.com: news, ranking, recruiting, rules, tips, camps

www.Insidelacrosse.com: high school, college, and pro news, recruiting info

www.Alllacrosseamerica.com: links, news, message boards, camps

www.Laxtips.com: text and audio tips from pro and college players

Volleyball

American Volleyball Coaches Association (www.avca.org)

www.Volleyball.com: forums, coaches corner, links

www.Volleyball.org: international, high school, college, and pro news

www.Cvu.com: collegiate scores, standings, news, links

www.Usavolleyball.org: news, events, camps, rules

Swimming

American Swimming Coaches Association (www.swimmingcoach.org)

www.Cscaa.org: College Swimming Coaches Association of America

www.Nisca.net: National Interscholastic Swimming Coaches Association

www.Swimnews.com: news, results, forums, links

Skiing

www.Usskiteam.com: United States Ski Team

www.Skinet.com: news, links, merchandise

Football

American Football Coaches Association (www.afca.org)

www.Ncaafootball.net: news and results for all divisions

www.Thefootballportal.com: football-related links

www.Football-links.com: football-related links

www.Nflhs.com: NFL high school news, tips, drills

Finish Line

Take some time to go through the requirements at each of the levels to see where you fit. If you haven't already, register with the NCAA Clearinghouse. You can also use the division lists by sport on the following pages to locate some schools you might have previously overlooked in building your Target List.

Forms You'll Need and References You'll Use

In this chapter:

- ☐ Checklists to guide you through each year of high school
- ☐ Sample correspondence and profile
- ☐ Useful websites
- ☐ Form to help you identify your top school
- ☐ Charts for figuring costs and your family contribution

This chapter serves as a catchall for the topics that were covered earlier in the book. Here you'll find useful tools to help you through the recruiting process.

Checklist

Freshman School Year and Summer

ACADEMIC

- ☐ Take the most challenging courses you can handle.
- ☐ Meet your guidance counselor and let him know of your desire to compete in college.
- ☐ Make sure he knows that you must meet the core course requirement.

☐ Work hard at school and strive for a 4.0 GPA.

☐ Learn to manage your time and develop good study habits.

☐ Visit any college campuses you can. The best choices are your parents' alma maters and the schools of relatives, siblings, and friends currently attending college.

ATHLETICS

☐ Attend a college game.

☐ Purchase instructional tapes to help you improve your skills.

☐ Start a weight-lifting program (ask your trainer for advice).

☐ Stay in shape year-round.

☐ Compete for your high school team.

☐ Compete for a summer club team.

☐ Attend a summer camp.

Sophomore School Year and Summer

ACADEMIC

☐ Make a commitment to improve your grades and take challenging courses.

☐ Meet with your guidance counselor to make sure you are taking classes to satisfy your core course requirement and are staying on track.

☐ Hire a tutor, form a study group with your friends, and seek extra help from your teachers to improve your GPA.

☐ Start researching various careers in which you might have interest in order to give you an idea of potential college majors.

☐ Make a preliminary Target List. Include as many schools as possible.

☐ Take the PSAT in October so that you know where you need to improve.

☐ Visit more college campuses.

ATHLETICS

☐ Make unofficial visits to as many schools on your Target List as possible.

☐ Stay in shape year-round by running and lifting weights (ask your school's trainer to design a program for you).

☐ Compete on your high school team.

☐ Attend a winter camp specifically for your event.

Junior School Year and Summer

ACADEMIC

☐ Make a commitment to improve your grades and take challenging courses.

☐ Start compiling a Target List of schools that interest you both academically and athletically. Consider the schools you have visited, and draw on the experiences of your parents, siblings, and family friends.

☐ Meet with your guidance counselor to make sure you are taking classes to satisfy your core course requirements and to get advice on your Target List.

☐ Enroll in a prep course such as Kaplan or Princeton Review to help you achieve the highest possible SAT/ACT score.

☐ Take the *U.S. News* webpage survey to help identify schools that meet your needs.

☐ Speak with your parents and family friends about their college experiences.

☐ Review your Target List of schools monthly to remove or add schools.

☐ Read college catalogs and webpages of schools you are considering.

☐ Take the PSAT again in October.

☐ Take the SAT/ACT in the spring.

ATHLETICS

☐ Register with the NCAA Clearinghouse.

☐ Call each college division to request a copy of their student-athlete guide so that you are familiar with all rules and regulations.

☐ Attend as many games of schools on your Target List as you can.

☐ Send letters of interest and your player profile to coaches on your Target List, preferably before your high school season starts.

☐ Ask your high school coach, club, summer coach, or influential athletes who have seen you compete to send letters of recommendation to schools on your Target List.

☐ Complete and return college questionnaires promptly.

☐ Seek opinions from high school coaches and other qualified persons concerning your ability to compete in college sports.

☐ Make unofficial visits to as many schools on your Target List as possible.

☐ Meet with the head coach of any school you visit.

☐ Publish your personal website and promote it to college coaches.

☐ Seek national exposure by competing in national or regional competitions and showcases and by attending summer camps at your top-choice schools.

☐ Attend a Christmas-break camp if it does not conflict with your winter-sport season.

☐ Stay in shape year-round by running and lifting weights (ask your school's trainer to design a program for you).

☐ Begin to concentrate on your best position.

☐ Compete in top summer leagues or competitive clubs.

Senior School Year and Summer

ACADEMIC

☐ Retake the SAT/ACT.

☐ Compare your GPA with your SAT/ACT score and the qualifier index.

☐ Retake the SAT/ACT if your scores need improvement.

☐ In September, request a copy of *Meeting College Costs* from your guidance office to determine how much money you need for college.

☐ Ask for teacher recommendations.

☐ Finalize your Target List and apply to these schools.

☐ Meet all application and financial aid deadlines.

☐ Evaluate your college options, and consider scholarship and financial offers.

☐ Inform each college to which you've been accepted of your final decision.

ATHLETICS

- ☐ Call each college division to request a copy of their student-athlete guide so that you are familiar with all rules and regulations (the guides are updated yearly, so you want to stay abreast of any changes).

- ☐ Make unofficial and official visits to schools on your Target List.

- ☐ Train year-round.

- ☐ Attend a winter camp.

- ☐ Increase your lifting program.

- ☐ Compete at national and regional events.

- ☐ Contact your coach for a summer training program.

Correspondence

The purpose of this section is to help you think of ideas for your correspondence with college coaches. Do not copy any of these letters word for word. Make sure you write your own versions so that you stand out from the crowd. Also, many coaches are familiar with this guide, and it will look bad for you if they notice you plagiarized it.

Tips

- Type long letters, but handwrite shorter ones if your writing is neat and legible. It will be more personal than if you type them (you can type your player profile).

- Individualize your letters—do not send the same version to multiple schools. If a coach suspects that you sent a bulk mailing, he will not give your letter as much attention.

- Use stationery to give your correspondence a professional appearance. You can design your own version on a computer using a nice font. Include your name, address, phone, and e-mail.

- Do not call or mail letters to a college coach at his house unless he gives you permission. It's rude and you may annoy him. Always use the coach's office as your contact point.

- Send letters promptly. A thank-you note received the day after a meeting makes a much better impression than one received two weeks later.

Hold Up

Coaches Evaluate the "Little Things" Too!

Bob Temple, VarisityPages.com

Everything you do, and everything you send to a college coach, reflect on you. This includes some of the little things that many people may not think about.

My company recently needed to hire a large number of writers to help out with a specific project. To do this, I placed an advertisement for freelance writers on a popular job-search site. The response to the ad was tremendous. There were hundreds of writers who sent their resumes (just as there might be hundreds of athletes interested in being recruited by a college coach). In going through those communications, I weeded out candidates based primarily on their qualifications, of course. But little things also played a role.

One such little thing was a particular writer's e-mail address. Before I even got a chance to look at his cover letter or resume, I noticed that his e-mail address was a reference to his favorite alcoholic beverage. When he created this e-mail address, he probably thought it was funny. But using it in a business context was inappropriate.

So, if your primary e-mail address might give a negative impression (budman@xyz.com or bigmanoncampus@xyz.com, for example), you might want to consider changing it or using a different one to communicate with coaches.

Bob Temple is a sports writer who has covered all the major professional sports leagues, major college sports, and high school sports throughout a seventeen-year writing career. He's also authored seven Internet-related books (two on sports topics) and more than twenty children's nonfiction books (eight on sports topics).

Letter of Interest

PURPOSE: To let a college coach know you are interested in competing for his team. Discuss your academic interests and request literature on the school and team.

Athlete Profile

PURPOSE: To highlight your academic and athletic accomplishments in an easy-to-read format. Include personal, athletic, and academic information; references; and a photo of you in your uniform. This should accompany the letter of interest.

Letter Accompanying a Highlight Video

PURPOSE: To introduce your highlight video and encourage the coach to watch it. Mention that you are sending the video because the coach asked for one. Do not send a video unless a coach requests it.

Thank-You Note after a Campus Visit

PURPOSE: To thank a coach for taking the time to meet with you, to discuss the possibility of competing for his team, and to let him know you are still interested in being recruited. Include specific examples of something pertaining to your meeting so the coach remembers you.

Letter Providing New Information

PURPOSE: To inform a coach of new developments and reinforce your desire to be recruited. You can send a copy of your game schedule, let the coach know that you will be competing in a prestigious event, or inform him that you just made the dean's list.

Jason Kline
10324 Town Walk Dr.
Yorktown Heights, NY 10598
Phone: 718-555-1000 E-mail: jumpshot7@aol.com

September 12, 2004

Mr. Keith Kessinger
Head Basketball Coach
Carson-Newman College
2130 Branner Avenue
Jefferson City, TN 37760

Dear Coach Kessinger:

After I graduate from Yorktown H.S. this June, I am interested in attending Carson-Newman College. My goal is to graduate with a premed degree from your prestigious McCarthur School. I am writing to express interest in attending your school and, more specifically, playing basketball next year.

As a three-year captain of my high school basketball team, I have developed the skills and leadership ability to contribute to your nationally ranked squad. Last season I was nominated to the All-Section Team while leading my team in points per game (27) and assists (11).

My interest in Carson-Newman College has always been strong—I have had the opportunity to attend seven of your games. In fact, two alumni from my high school, Jim Nicholson and Spencer Davis, played for your team in the late 1990s.

Attached is a player profile that details my academic and athletic accomplishments. You'll notice that I take my studies just as seriously as I do basketball, and I'm confident that I will represent your program with distinction.

Please add my name to your prospect list and send me information about Carson-Newman's track program. I would especially like to see a copy of your media guide.

Good luck this season.

Go Eagles!

Sincerely yours,

Jason

Jason Kline

JASON KLINE	FORWARD	CLASS '05

Address: 10324 Town Walk Dr.
Phone: 914-555-1000   E-mail: jumpshot7@aol.com
DOB: June 24, 1986
Height: 6'4" Weight: 165 lbs.
SS#   102-24-2422

ACADEMIC
High School: Yorktown High School
                  17 Green Road
                  Yorktown Heights, NY 10598
                  914-232-9444
Graduation: Class of 2005
GPA: 3.8 GPA (on a 4.0 scale)
SAT: 1240 total (600 math, 640 verbal)
Class rank: Top 10%
Honors: National Merit Scholar
                  2nd place County Science Fair Competition
                  Student Volunteer of the Month—Mothers Against Drunk Driving
Counselor: Jim Ryan (ext. 343)

HIGH SCHOOL BASKETBALL
Coach   Jim Dobbs (ext. 432)
Awards: Basketball—All League
                  Team Captain—'02–'03
2002 stats: • 27 points/game
                  • 11 assists/game
                  • 7 rebounds/game

REFERENCES
Summer coach Jim Haas (718-232-9453)
Trainer   Lasse Viren (212-555-2234)
Teacher   Deborah Klein (ext. 232)—English AP
Employer   Calvin Hobbs—McDonald's (718-343-3453)
Volunteer mgr. Stacey Jackson—Mothers Against Drunk Driving (718-343-9343)

Handwrite these letters on your stationery and use the same layout as in the letter of interest.

Thank-You Note after a Campus Visit

Dear Coach Kessinger:

Thank you for taking time to meet with me during my visit to Carson-Newman College last Saturday. I really enjoyed touring the campus, attending a science class, and speaking with you about your basketball team. It gave me a great glimpse of what I can expect at college next fall. I can't wait!

I'm glad I got a chance to see your team play. I was impressed with the talent of your squad, the team unity, and competitive spirit of your players. I can definitely see myself wearing the Blue and Gold!

Thanks again for your hospitality and for your interest in recruiting me.

Letter Providing New Information

Dear Coach Kessinger:

I want to let you know that my high school basketball team will be competing at the Nike High School Invitational in Tampa, Florida, December 7–10. If any of your assistant coaches are covering the event, I'd really appreciate it if they could watch me play. Enclosed is the schedule. I'll be wearing #32.

By the way, I just found out that I made the honor roll for the third semester in a row, and my research project on solar energy won third prize in our county science fair. My hard work is paying off!

Thanks again for considering me for your '05 recruiting class.

Internet Sites

The web offers a wealth of college-related resources, from free test-prep courses to loan calculators to statistics on campus crime. But you should surf carefully. Some sites accept fees from colleges to list their schools prominently. Others require you to register and will sell your personal information to marketers if you neglect to sign complicated privacy agreements.

Moreover, when researching colleges online it's important to dig deep and think critically. Many colleges have spent thousands of dollars on fancy websites that are little more than glitzy ads.

College Board (www.collegeboard.com)

Collegeboard.com is one of the most comprehensive sites. It produces a customized roster of schools for students who answer questions on everything from dorms to school size. The site also contains other important information relating to the SATs and AP tests. For instance, the site lists schools that allow students with one year's worth of AP or International Baccalaureate credits to skip a year of college. In addition, it includes a free, searchable scholarship database called "LikeFinder."

U.S. News & World Report (www.usnews.com)

Catch This
Once a search engine has spit out a list of possible schools, you typically can click straight to each college's home page. In the past couple of years, these pages have become a popular source of information about colleges, ordering course catalogs, sample financial aid packages, and virtual campus tours.
But students should bear in mind that much of the material on these sites is promotional. The *Internet Guide for College-Bound Students* encourages students not only to browse the "official" pages, such as the virtual tour, but to ferret out "unofficial" information as well.

Their search creates a list of potential schools based on your answers to questions about cost, geographic location, major, and several other preferences. The site features college rankings so that you can identify schools according to the criteria that matter most to you, such as student-to-faculty ratio or acceptance rate. Another tool is the personality quiz. Rate the validity of eighty statements, including "I want to be able to contribute to society someday" and "Friends and I enjoy discussing intellectual ideas," to find out the kinds of colleges where you'll feel at home. Need help whittling down your list? Chat with counselors and other experts on the forum or compare the stats of up to four schools.

Princeton Review (www.review.com)

More hip but more commercial is Princeton Review's site. Its Counselor-O-Matic poses glib questions about your academic performance and interests. Then the site produces a list of colleges divided into "safety," "good match," and "reach" schools. It also has college admission discussion boards, but you have to register to participate.

Apply Online

Once you have your final Target List, the Internet can make the process of applying a little easier. Many college sites have applications that either can be printed and filled out by hand or completed electronically. In addition, you can log on to one of several sites devoted to e-applications. In most cases, the services are free, although students still have to pay an application fee to the schools.

Some of them—such as www.collegelink.com (a web partner of *U.S. News* online), www.xap.com, and www.collegenet.com—host hundreds of colleges' applications, which can be filled out and submitted electronically. Students also can turn to www.commonapp.org for a generic form, called the common application, which is accepted by 209 colleges.

But don't let the relative ease of applying electronically be your downfall. Too often, students who would take care with a paper form hurry through online applications. If you decide to apply online, be sure to have a parent or teacher read over your essays before you hit the submit button.

Financial Aid (www.ed.gov/studentaid)

One of the first sites you will want to visit in your search for college funds is the Department of Education's federal student financial aid home page. The government gives grants, loans, and work-study assistance to more than ten million students each year, and if you want to be among their ranks, you'll need to fill out their Free Application for Federal Student Aid, or FAFSA. The site provides so much detailed information, however, that it can put you to sleep.

For a jazzier discussion of federal programs, check out www.finaid.org. This site also offers calculators to help you figure out how much you will get from the government and how long it will take to pay the loans back. While numerous sites provide searchable scholarship databases, stay clear of those that charge you money or "guarantee" that you'll win a scholarship; scholarship scams are prevalent.

Loans (www.wiredscholar.com)

One of the best funding information sites is run by Sallie Mae, the largest private education loan company. Easy to navigate and without registration requirements, the site has a database of hundreds of thousands of scholarships worth over a billion dollars. Why does the firm offer the site? To acquire new loan customers. In other words, if you don't find a scholarship, a private loan is just a click away.

Scholarship Database (www.fastweb.com)

With over six hundred thousand awards, FastWeb is one of the most aggressive in updating its scholarship database. To use the search, however, you must submit to a lengthy registration process that includes solicitations that pop up between questions. FastWeb sells registered users' names to banks and universities, and those who don't want their names released must indicate this at the beginning of the registration process.

Athletic Scholarships (www.athleticscholarships.net)

Their athletic scholarship recruiting service can help you apply for college athletic scholarships. Their service covers all NCAA and NAIA sports.

Social Life (www.collegenews.com)

To get the skinny on the social life at a particular college, check out this site, which also has a complete listing of college newspapers.

Proofreading Application Essays (www.essayedge.com)

Also worth a click is EssayEdge, a site that offers a wealth of free material on writing college essays. For a fee, their experts also will read and edit your essay.

Test Prep (www.testu.com)

TestU charges $50 for an online program based on your strengths and weaknesses. Another site, www.Number2.com, takes the democratization of test prep further by offering a free interactive course.

Not to be outdone, last year both Kaplan and Princeton Review introduced online courses, as well as free minicourses. And even the College Board—which sponsors the SAT—has gotten in on the act with free and low-cost test prep.

Crime Reports (www.ope.ed.gov/security)

This is a good source to find out about a school's safety record. Think critically about what you read. When institutions report crime data, they use different definitions of offenses, so some direct comparisons among campuses may not be valid.

College Net (www.collegenet.com)

A matching service that helps you find your ideal school and online applications from over fifteen hundred colleges.

Preparing Your Child for College (www.ed.gov/studentaid)

Helps your parents with general college concerns.

Peterson's Education Center (www.petersons.com)

A leading provider of college entrance exam preparation.

CollegeBound Magazine (www.collegebound.net)

Informative magazine articles to help with issues facing incoming freshmen. Subscriptions available.

College Apps (www.collegeapps.com)

Collegeapps.com shows college-bound students how to personalize that very sterile college application form and market themselves to gain admission.

Collegenet (www.collegenet.com)

Provides here for your convenience over fifteen hundred customized Internet admission applications built for college and university programs. When applying to more than one program, you save redundant typing since common data automatically travels from form to form.

Go College (www.gocollege.com)

Find your dream school, learn how to apply, search for the perfect match. Offers great tips on financial aid, scholarships, SATs, and ACTs.

Get Recruited (www.get-recruited.com)

Helps make the college recruiting process work for students and institutions of higher education. Brings students together with colleges, universities, graduate schools, and professional schools and helps them identify the scholarships and financial aid for which they may qualify.

A-Game (www.a-game.com)

This site is here to help you play your A-game—not just in your sport but also in the classroom. They want to help you take advantage of the opportunities—and avoid the dangers—in sports, school, and life.

Youth Baseball Coaching (www.youthbaseballcoaching.com)

Portal of college recruiting, scholarship, and academic links related to, but not limited to, baseball.

College Link (www.collegelink.com)

Assists you with searching for colleges, applying, and making your final college decision.

Financial Aid Information Page (www.finaid.org)

Answers all questions about financial aid, loans, scholarships, and military aid.

Scholarships (www.scholarships.com)

Scholarship finder and general information about financial aid.

Financial Aid (www.fafsa.ed.gov)

An online version of the Free Application for Federal Student Aid

Mapping Your Future (www.mapping-your-future.org)

Helps you plan a career after college.

Career Resource Center (www.careers.org)

Assists with career advice and planning.

National Student Loan Data System (www.nslds.ed.gov)

The U.S. Department of Education's central database for student aid that receives data from schools, agencies that guarantee loans, the Direct Loan program, the Pell Grant program, and others.

National Soccer Coaches Association of America (www.nscaa.com)

Founded in 1941, the NSCAA is the largest coaches' organization in the United States. The organization provides an extensive awards program for over ten thousand individuals and also provides national rankings for high school and colleges.

National Field Hockey Coaches Association (www.eteamz.com/NFHCA)

Provides a recognizable presence and voice in regard to legislation affecting the sport of field hockey as well as interscholastic and intercollegiate programs.

Intercollegiate Women's Lacrosse Coaches Association (www.iwlca.org)

The IWLCA is the peak national body for women's lacrosse in the United States. Its mission is to foster and develop the sport nationwide.

United States Intercollegiate Lacrosse Association (www.usila.org)

Sponsors rankings of the top collegiate teams and provides information and news on the latest developments in college lacrosse.

American Baseball Coaches Association (www.abca.org)

Even though this site is geared to college coaches, it features instructional articles, national poll results, and interesting feature stories.

High School Track Web (www.hstrackweb.com)

Comprehensive information geared to high school runners, featuring recruiting articles, how-to information, interviews with college coaches, message boards, and listings of over one thousand websites of high school track teams.

National High School Track Coaches Association (www.trackcoaches.org)

Provides services and recognition for high school coaches and helps promote and represent high school track.

National Collegiate Athletic Association (www.ncaa.org)

Represents 1,024 four-year schools in three divisions (I, II, and III).

National Athletic of Intercollegiate Athletics (www.naia.org)

Represents 180 four-year schools.

National Junior College Athletic Association (www.njcaa.org)

Represents 503 two-year programs representing three divisions (I, II, and III).

American Volleyball Coaches Assistant (www.avca.org)

Although most services focus on volleyball coaches, the organization's website has a comprehensive listing of camps available for searching. The AVCA is based in Colorado Springs, Colorado.

USA Water Polo (www.usawaterpolo.com)

Provides valuable content on current collegiate programs and players and upcoming tournaments and championships.

Women's Basketball Coaches Association (www.wbca.org)

Provides information on collegiate programs as well as coaches. In addition, the organization sponsors an all-star game for talented high school seniors and provides listings of camps and clinics.

National Association of Basketball Coaches (www.nabc.org)

Provides comprehensive news about men's college basketball, including useful links that update the latest developments in recruiting trends.

National Collegiate Bowling Coaches Association (www.ncbca.org)

Primarily for coaches, provides a list of where the top collegiate players are located and which programs consistently produce the best players.

United States Fencing (www.usfencing.org)

Provides information about individual tournaments and competitions as well as a national ranking scheme.

American Hockey Coaches Association (www.ahca.org)

Provides information on awards programs for collegiate players and has bibliographic information on a variety of college coaches.

American Women's Hockey Coaches Association (www.awhca.org)

Information on women's hockey awards programs and bibliographic information on a variety of college coaches.

College Swimming Coaches of America Association (www.cscaa.org)

Gives access to top collegiate swimming times, teams, coaches, and athletes in the NCAA (Divisions I, II, III) and the NAIA.

College Golf Foundation (www.cgfgolf.org)

Provides a rating scheme for collegiate programs, organizes college tournaments, and providing a comprehensive list of links dealing with collegiate golf.

College Tennis Online (www.collegetennisonline.com)

Primarily filled with news content and scores, this site also provides links to college camps, collegiate teams, and program rankings.

Online College Questionnaires

Filling out an online college questionnaire is a quick and effective way for you to show your interest in a particular school. Online questionnaires allow potential student athletes to give coaches a brief overview of who they are and what they want to accomplish.

Although questionnaires can be filled out quickly online, it is important that you not take them for granted. These forms are seen as a reflection of who you are, so answer each question with well-thought-out answers.

Guidelines to Keep in Mind When Filling Out Online College Questionnaires

Proofread at least twice: By putting extra effort into ensuring the copy you send a perspective coach is well written and error-free, you are sending a message that you are detail oriented, responsible, and motivated.

It is never too early: Fill in questionnaires as soon as you place a school on your Target List. The earlier you complete a questionnaire, the sooner you get your name to your top-choice schools.

Do your homework: Where possible on the questionnaire, demonstrate your strong interest in the school. Include specific classes, professors, or other attributes of the college or university that interest you.

College Information Sheet

The best way to keep your college materials organized is to print this sheet for each school on your Target List. Place each sheet—along with any school catalogs or other information you receive—inside a file folder. Write the school's name on the outside of the folder.

General

School _____ Division: _____

Address _____ City _____ State _____ Zip _____

Admissions dept. phone _____ Webpage _____

Academics

Academic rating: ☐ Most competitive ☐ Average ☐ Less competitive ☐ Not competitive

Potential major/departments of interest _____

Prestige of degree: ☐ Very prestigious ☐ Average ☐ Not prestigious

Undergraduate enrollment _____ Faculty:student ratio _____

Average GPA of accepted applicants _____ Average SAT/ACT scores _____

Likelihood of being accepted: ☐ Safety school ☐ Likely ☐ Reach

Conversation notes with admissions department (include date and what you discussed)

_____

_____

Athletics

Head coach _____ Recruiting coordinator _____

Assistant coaches _____

Athletic office phone_____ E-mail addresses_____

Coach's interest: ☐ Recruiting me heavily ☐ Slight interest ☐ No discussions yet ☐ None

Athletes in my sport _____ How many recruited at my position _____

Likelihood of contributing: ☐ Definitely ☐ Maybe ☐ Slim chance

Been to a game? _____ Compete on TV? _____

Does coach want me to redshirt? ☐ Yes ☐ No   Graduation rate of athletes: _____

Scholarship offered? ☐ No ☐ Yes—amount _____

Competitive schedule? ☐ Yes ☐ No   Overnight trips: ☐ Yes ☐ No

Offered an official visit: ☐ No ☐ Yes—when _____

Unofficial visit planned? ☐ No ☐ Yes—when _____

Athletic facilities (fields, weight room): ☐ Excellent ☐ Average ☐ Poor

Strength of team/schedule: ☐ Excellent ☐ Average ☐ Weak

Conversation notes with coaches (include date and what you discussed)

_____

_____

Finances

Tuition _____   Room and board _____   Transportation to/from home _____

How much of a financial aid/scholarship package do I need to afford this school? _____

Conversation notes with financial aid department (include date and what you discussed)

_____

_____

Other Considerations

Housing: ☐ On-campus dorm ☐ Off-campus apartment

Campus life: ☐ Lots of activities ☐ Average ☐ Little to do
Greek Life: ☐ Big ☐ Average ☐ None

Transportation home: ☐ Fly—duration of trip _____ ☐ Drive—duration of trip _____

Friends, relatives, or high school alumni who have gone to this school: _____

Would I be happy at this school if I didn't play sports? ☐ Yes ☐ No

Identify Your Number 1 School

If you have trouble selecting a school that you want to attend, complete this exercise after you receive your acceptance letters.

1. Specify how important each of the following criteria is by checking one of the three boxes labeled *very*, *somewhat*, or *not*. This will help focus your decision.
2. Rank what you think is *very important* to you on a scale of 1–5 (5 being best).
3. Add up all the rankings. If this doesn't clearly identify your number 1 choice, then you can rank all the criteria that you believe is *somewhat important*.

IMPORTANCE TO ME?

Very	Somewhat	Not	Criteria	SCHOOL #1 (_____)	SCHOOL #2 (_____)	SCHOOL #3 (_____)
			Academics			
☐	☐	☐	School's reputation	_____	_____	_____
☐	☐	☐	Fields of study	_____	_____	_____
☐	☐	☐	Prestige of degree	_____	_____	_____
☐	☐	☐	Professors	_____	_____	_____
☐	☐	☐	Class size	_____	_____	_____
☐	☐	☐	Alumni network	_____	_____	_____
☐	☐	☐	Small enrollment	_____	_____	_____
☐	☐	☐	In-state	_____	_____	_____
☐	☐	☐	Out-of-state	_____	_____	_____
☐	☐	☐	Athletic tutoring	_____	_____	_____
			Athletics			
☐	☐	☐	Scholarships	_____	_____	_____
☐	☐	☐	Chance to play	_____	_____	_____
☐	☐	☐	High-profile team/conf.	_____	_____	_____
☐	☐	☐	Transfer opportunities	_____	_____	_____
☐	☐	☐	Caliber of team	_____	_____	_____
☐	☐	☐	Competitive schedule	_____	_____	_____
☐	☐	☐	Coaching staff	_____	_____	_____
☐	☐	☐	Athletic facilities	_____	_____	_____
☐	☐	☐	Graduation rate	_____	_____	_____

Other

				School #1	School #2	School #3
☐	☐	☐	My parents approve	_____	_____	_____
☐	☐	☐	Location	_____	_____	_____
☐	☐	☐	Climate	_____	_____	_____
☐	☐	☐	Greek life	_____	_____	_____
☐	☐	☐	Distance from home	_____	_____	_____
☐	☐	☐	Campus events	_____	_____	_____
☐	☐	☐	Social life	_____	_____	_____
☐	☐	☐	Meet new people	_____	_____	_____
☐	☐	☐	Out-of-pocket cost	_____	_____	_____
			Grand total	_____	_____	_____

Cost-of-College Comparison

EXPENSES	SCHOOL #1	SCHOOL #2	SCHOOL #3
	(_____)	(_____)	(_____)
Tuition and fees	_____	_____	_____
Room and board	_____	_____	_____
Books and supplies	_____	_____	_____
Personal expenses	_____	_____	_____
Transportation	_____	_____	_____
Other	_____	_____	_____
TOTAL EXPENSES	_____	_____	_____
TOTAL FINANCIAL AID	_____	_____	_____
YOUR ANNUAL COST	_____	_____	_____

(Total expenses minus total financial aid)

Estimated Family Contribution

This chart provides an approximation of how much financial aid departments will expect your family to contribute toward your college expenses each year. The figures are based on only one parent working, no other siblings in college, and no unusual financial circumstances. You should also add a $700–$1,000 student contribution to the final amount. These figures are only estimates. Your actual contribution may vary.

	Net Assets of $20,000				Net Assets of $40,000			
Family size	3	4	5	6	3	4	5	6
Income before taxes								
8,000	—	—	—	—	—	—	—	—
12,000	—	—	—	—	—	—	—	—
16,000	266	—	—	—	562	72	—	—
20,000	916	398	—	—	1,176	687	228	—
24,000	1,567	1,049	563	13	1,804	1,302	843	323
28,000	2,296	1,700	1,214	663	2,544	1,947	1,458	937
32,000	3,216	2,471	1,888	1,314	3,451	2,709	2,124	1,552
36,000	4,388	3,420	2,688	2,001	4,636	3,674	2,935	2,231
40,000	5,546	4,616	3,711	2,824	5,784	4,864	3,958	3,061
44,000	6,621	5,691	4,276	3,852	6,869	5,639	5,076	4,091
48,000	7,834	6,895	6,031	5,035	8,072	7,143	6,278	5,283
52,000	9,027	8,098	7,234	6,238	9,276	8,346	7,482	6,487
56,000	11,018	9,301	8,437	7,442	10,428	9,549	8,685	7,690
60,000	11,252	10,384	9,583	8,645	11,500	10,633	9,831	8,893

	Net Assets of $60,000				Net Assets of $80,000			
Family size	3	4	5	6	3	4	5	6
Income before taxes								
8,000	—	—	—	—	314	—	—	—
12,000	417	—	—	—	999	493	—	—
16,000	1,090	600	139	—	1,618	1,128	1,284	130
20,000	1,706	1,215	756	236	2,316	1,750	916	784
24,000	2,430	1,848	1,371	851	3,183	2,481	1,927	1,379
28,000	3,317	2,585	2,025	1,456	4,265	3,376	2,686	2,034
32,000	4,451	3,517	2,801	2,133	5,579	4,533	3,643	2,813
36,000	5,764	4,718	3,800	2,947	6,892	5,846	4,866	3,814
40,000	6,922	5,992	5,051	3,972	8,050	7,120	6,179	5,068
44,000	7,997	7,067	6,204	5,208	9,125	8,195	7,332	6,336
48,000	9,200	8,271	7,407	6,411	10,328	9,399	8,535	7,539
52,000	10,404	9,474	8,610	7,615	11,532	10,602	9,738	8,743
56,000	11,556	10,677	9,813	8,818	12,684	11,805	10,941	9,946
60,000	12,620	11,761	10,959	10,021	13,756	12,889	12,087	11,149

Finish Line

The forms and checklists in this section can be used by different people at different stages of the process. Begin with the checklists at the beginning of the chapter. Even if you're a junior already, go back through the freshman and sophomore checklists and determine if you completed all the items. Then bring yourself up to date to your current class.

Begin working on your correspondence. Check out some of the websites listed, and use the other forms as appropriate.

Glossary of Terms

ACT (American College Test) A curriculum-based college admission test. The multiple-choice questions that test English, mathematics, reading, and science reasoning on the ACT are a measure of what you've learned in your high school classes rather than a measure of aptitude or IQ. ACT results are accepted by most U.S. colleges.

advanced placement (AP) courses High school courses that can result in college credit, depending on your final exam score. AP courses are generally looked on favorably by college admissions officers as evidence of a challenging high school program.

athletic scholarship A form of financial aid that can be used to pay for tuition and fees, room and board, and books. It can be guaranteed for only one year at a time and must be renewed each year. Many coaches will verbally commit to and honor a four- or five-year scholarship even though they cannot put it in writing.

award letter A statement sent to you by a college that has accepted you; the letter recaps the amount and type of aid the college can offer.

blue-chip recruit A highly sought-after high school athlete who attracts the attention of a variety of high-profile college coaches and pro scouts. This gifted player possesses outstanding athletic ability, a tremendous work ethic, and generally excellent academic marks.

booster This person is usually a wealthy alumnus of the school with close ties to the athletic department. You will be ineligible for college athletics if you have any recruiting contact with boosters or alumni not employed by the college.

bylaw 14.3 NCAA D-I and D-II legislation that requires you to meet minimum GPA and SAT/ACT scores, take certain core courses, and graduate from high school before you can play college sports.

California Community Colleges (CCC) A small college division featuring fourteen junior colleges in California. These schools do not offer scholarships.

College Board A not-for-profit organization that administers many standardized tests, including the PSAT, SAT, SAT II, and AP. Additionally, the College Board offers official test-prep materials, a scholarship search, a personal inventory tool, and educational loans.

commercial loans or private/alternative loans Commercial loans are available through several financial services providers. To qualify, you must pass a credit check, and the interest rate will be higher than that of a Direct or FFEL Stafford or Perkins Loan. For these reasons, it is wise to investigate low-interest, federally sponsored options before applying for a commercial loan. In addition, beware of scholarship scams that are simply commercial loans in disguise.

community college See *junior college.*

contact Any face-to-face meeting in excess of a greeting between you and a college coach or a member of the athletic department. You may be contacted off campus only after July 1 before your senior year. Coaches may not contact you off campus more than three times.

co-op An education that integrates classroom study with paid, supervised work experiences. These jobs are part- or full-time and may lead to academic credit.

core courses Specified college preparatory courses that you need to take while in high school in order to be an eligible NCAA recruit.

direct expenses The total cost of tuition and fees, room and board, and books.

early signing period One week in mid-November during which you can sign a national letter of intent.

electronic application An alternative to traditional paper applications, electronic applications can take several forms. Some schools allow you to print application forms from their website or a CD-ROM, which you can fill in by hand and mail to the admissions office. Other schools support online applications that you can fill out and submit over the web. If you decide to apply electronically, you won't have to wait to receive materials in the mail. Best of all, applying electronically will get your application in the hands of admissions officers sooner.

evaluations Any off-campus activity used to assess your athletic ability. A coach may evaluate you at your high school or any other venue. NCAA D-III schools are not permitted to arrange an evaluation of you.

expected family contribution (EFC) The total you are expected to contribute toward the cost of college. The federal government determines the amount of your EFC based on the information you supply on the FAFSA and the total cost of attendance for the college of your choice. The total cost includes tuition, room and board, books, transportation, and other personal expenses. You will fill out the FAFSA each year, which may alter the EFC for each year of college.

financial aid package Each college has its own custom package, which may include federal and state grants, independent sources, school scholarships, student loans, and on-campus jobs. This provides you with a comparison guide among schools on your Target List.

Free Application for Federal Student Aid (FAFSA) The FAFSA is used to apply for federal student financial aid, including grants, loans, and work-study. In addition, it is used by most schools to award nonfederal student financial aid. The form is a summary of your family's financial situation, including income, debt, and assets for both you and your parents. You will have to fill out the FAFSA every year that you are in college.

family contribution The amount of money your family is expected to pay toward the student expense budget. This amount is a fixed sum determined by the federal methodology, and it will be the same regardless of what school you apply to.

Federal Family Education Loan (FFEL) program Low-interest education loans made by private lenders to students and parents. These loans may be either subsidized or unsubsidized, and there are several repayment plans available.

Federal Supplemental Educational Opportunity Grants (FSEOG) Government-sponsored, college-administered loans awarded to exceptionally needy students. Eligibility is determined by the federal government, and the program gives priority to students receiving federal support.

fellowships Fellowships are available to students in most disciplines, and they are sponsored by colleges and a range of organizations and institutions. Fellowships offered by organizations are often allocated in monthly stipends and can usually be used at any university. Fellowships are more common at the graduate level, but some undergraduate fellowships do exist. Additionally, there may be grant and fellowship money available for specific research projects or study abroad. Contact your major department, financial aid office, or career center for more information.

financial aid Any type of assistance used to help you meet college costs. It is divided into two categories: gift aid (athletic and academic scholarships and grants) and self-help aid (loans and work-study).

full athletic scholarship, or full ride Terms used when the college pays 100 percent of the expenses. These are rare and are usually given only to blue-chip athletes.

good academic standing Maintaining at least a C average while in college.

grant aid This is the most sought-after type of financial aid because it does not have to be paid back. You may receive grant aid on the basis of either need or merit, and it may come from your school or the federal government. Federal grants include the need-based Pell and Federal Supplemental Educational Opportunity (FSEOG) Grants.

hook When you write your admission essays, you'll want to engage your readers quickly. Using your "hook," a unique personal trait or experience, is one way to achieve this goal. If you're a dedicated and accomplished cellist or have trekked through the Himalayas, these might make good starting points for college essays. Your hook will be something about you that's unique and interesting.

Hope credit A nonrefundable federal income tax credit equal to all of the first $1,000 out-of-pocket payments for qualified tuition and related expenses and 50 percent of the second $1,000, for a maximum $1,500 per student, per year. The

Hope credit applies to the first two years of postsecondary education. You may not claim both the Hope credit and the *Lifetime Learning credit* (see term).

indirect expenses The total cost of transportation to and from school, incidental expenses, and supplies.

Ivy League The athletic conference that boasts academic powerhouses Brown, Columbia, Cornell, Dartmouth, Harvard, Penn, Princeton, and Yale. Acceptance to an Ivy League school is considered the brass ring of the application process, although many argue that an equal, if not better, education can be achieved at many non–Ivy League schools.

junior college, or JC, or JUCO Represents all two-year schools, including community colleges. These schools provide college courses for recent high school graduates and adults in their communities. JCs generally have fewer admission requirements than four-year institutions do, and courses typically cost less than comparable courses at four-year schools. Many students use a JC as a springboard to a four-year college or U.

lab sciences High school science courses that supplement textbook study with hands-on experimentation. Examples include biology, chemistry, and physics. Other courses, such as economics, may be considered scientific disciplines but do not qualify as lab sciences. Consult your guidance counselor or your prospective college's admissions office for further details.

late signing period One week in mid-April during which you can sign a national letter of intent.

letter of intent (LOI) A four-page contract administered by the Collegiate Commissioners Association that commits you to attend a specific college. If you change your mind after signing the letter, you must be mutually released from your commitment by the old school and your new school. In addition, you cannot play for one year, and you lose a year of eligibility. This is a serious contract that should not be taken lightly.

Lifetime Learning credit The Lifetime Learning credit may be claimed for your tuition and related expenses on your parents' tax returns. Through 2002, the amount that may be claimed as a credit is equal to 20 percent of the taxpayer's first $5,000 of out-of-pocket qualified tuition and related expenses for all the students in the family for a maximum of $1,000. Individuals with modified adjusted gross incomes of $50,000 or more and joint filers with modified adjusted gross incomes of $100,000 or more are not eligible for the Lifetime Learning credit.

likely letter A letter sent to an athletic scholarship recipient in the fall or early winter that lets a student-athlete know the likelihood of being accepted to the school and the probable size of the financial package to be received.

merit-based aid, or merit scholarships Any form of financial aid not based on demonstrated financial need. Merit-based aid—which can take the form of grants, athletic or academic scholarships, or loans on favorable terms—is generally granted by each school and/or its alumni associations and wealthy benefactors. You may qualify for it by meeting a certain academic requirement, such as through GPA, test scores, a career goal, or an essay competition. Your financial aid package may include both need and merit-based aid.

National Association of Intercollegiate Athletics (NAIA) The NAIA represents smaller schools and can provide scholarships.

National Merit Scholarship A distinction award you can receive if you score high enough on the NMSQT/PSAT (National Merit Scholar Qualifying Test/Preliminary Scholastic Aptitude Test). The test may be administered for practice during your sophomore year, but only your junior-year score counts.

National Collegiate Athletic Association (NCAA) The main association for intercollegiate athletics, the NCAA is made up of three divisions—I, II, and III. Division I and II offer track scholarships.

National Junior College Athletic Association (NJCAA) The association that overseas two-year programs. The NJCAA is divided into three divisions—I, II, and III. Divisions I and II offer track scholarships. See also, *junior college*.

NCAA Clearinghouse An organization established by the NCAA that determines if you are eligible both for an official visit and for recruitment by NCAA D-I or D-II schools. You should register with the NCAA Clearinghouse at the start of your junior year of high school.

need-based aid If the cost of attendance for your college exceeds your expected family contribution (EFC), you will be eligible for need-based aid to cover the difference. You may be awarded a financial aid package that consists of a combination of grants, scholarships, loans, and work-study. The total amount of your package will be determined by a combination of demonstrated financial need, federal award maximums, and your school's available funds.

official visit Your trip to a college campus, paid in whole or in part by that institution. You are permitted by the NCAA to take one expense-paid visit to each of five schools that are recruiting you during your senior year, regardless of how many sports you play. Visits are limited to forty-eight hours. You must pay for all additional visits.

Parent Loans for Undergraduate Students (PLUS) and Supplemental Loans for Students (SLS) Two federal programs that assist families who don't qualify for need-based aid or who need help with their family contribution.

partial qualifier You can receive a scholarship and practice, but you many not play games during your first year of school. If you are able to complete your academic degree in four years, you may stay at school a fifth year, giving you four years of eligibility.

Patriot League The NCAA D-I athletic conference that includes Bucknell, U.S. Military Academy, Lehigh, U.S. Naval Academy, American University, Lafayette, and Holy Cross and does not offer track scholarships, except for American.

Pell Grants Given by the federal government, these grants are awarded to those students demonstrating exceptional financial need. Pell Grants do not need to be paid back.

Perkins Loans Awarded by each school, these low-interest loans (around 5 percent) are given to students who demonstrate exceptional financial need. Repayment of this loan begins nine months after you graduate, leave school, or drop to less than half-time student status.

Preliminary Standard Aptitude Test (PSAT) The PSAT is administered by the College Board. You may take the PSAT to familiarize yourself with the test and the kinds of questions you'll encounter on the SAT. The PSAT is also used as the qualifying test for the National Merit Scholar competition. This test is usually taken during your junior year of high school, but a practice PSAT may be given during your sophomore year. Like the SAT, the PSAT uses multiple-choice questions to test verbal and mathematical reasoning ability.

private counselors You may consult private counselors as you prepare to select and apply to colleges. They may operate as consultants or as employees of educational service providers such as Kaplan or the Princeton Review. Private counselors can help you assess your personality and academic needs to form a list of desirable college attributes. They can also help you figure out where and to how many schools you should apply. Private counselors can give you more attention than the average high school guidance counselor, but they can be pricey.

PROFILE The CSS/Financial Aid PROFILE is a customized financial aid application form required at certain colleges that collects additional financial information to determine eligibility for institutional aid.

Proposition 48 This law states that student-athletes must meet certain requirements if they want to practice and play during their freshman year at an NCAA Division I or Division II school.

prospective student-athlete Once you begin your freshmen year of high school, you may meet with college coaches but only if you initiate contact during an unofficial visit.

redshirt A term that describes you if you sit out a year of competition. If you are injured during your freshmen year or if your college coach believes that you need an extra year to develop, you may be "redshirted." You would be permitted to practice with the team, but you would not be allowed to play in games. Redshirt athletes must complete their four years of athletic eligibility within six years.

SAT II The SAT II assesses knowledge in various subject areas. Most colleges require the writing test, a math test, and a foreign language test. They are taken in the spring of your junior year and the fall of your senior year. If the test is linked to a specific subject, such as chemistry, it's best to take the test as soon as possible upon the completion of the course.

scholarship A type of financial aid that does not require repayment or employment and is usually awarded to students who demonstrate potential for academic or athletic achievement.

Scholastic Assessment Test (SAT) The SAT is administered by the College Board and is the most widely used college admission test. The SAT uses multiple-choice questions to assess verbal and mathematical reasoning ability. The SAT is taken during your junior or senior year. You may take this test multiple times if you wish to improve your score.

sliding scale A provision of the NCAA's bylaw 14.3 that calculates minimum GPA and SAT/ACT scores in order for you to be an eligible recruit. The higher your GPA, the lower your SAT/ACT requirement, and vice versa.

sports agent Someone who wants to handle all of your affairs (contract negotiation, sponsorships, financial planning, etc.) should you make it to the pros. You are in violation of NCAA rules if you agree to let a sports agent represent you while you are still in high school or college.

Stafford Loans These loans, both subsidized (need based) and unsubsidized (non–need based), are guaranteed by the federal government and are available to fund your education. Federal Stafford Loans are the most common source of education loan funds.

Student Aid Report (SAR) The official notification sent to you four to six weeks after filing the FAFSA. This report explains your EFC in relation to your school's expected cost of attendance. You may be required to submit this document to the financial aid office at the college you decide to attend.

student expense budget The total cost of attending a certain college for one academic year. Your financial need determined by the federal need analysis formula is the difference between the total coast of attending a college and your family's expected contribution.

student release form A document that you and your guidance counselor complete verifying your academic eligibility to compete at a NCAA D-I or D-II school.

subsidized loans Subsidized loans are based on financial need. With these loans, the interest is paid by the federal government until the repayment period begins and during authorized periods of deferment afterward.

test prep Preparing you for the college admission tests is big business. There are books, videos, CD-ROMs, and classroom courses you can purchase designed to help you do your best on the tests. It is wise to do some prep for the test. At a minimum, look over the informational packet about each test to familiarize yourself with the number and type of questions you'll be expected to answer. And don't expect miracles—you'll have to do some hard work to make any kind of test prep successful.

Title IX Also referred to as gender equity, this law mandates that institutions that receive federal funding, among other things, are not allowed to discriminate on the basis of sex. This means that schools have had to increase funding and opportunities for women's athletics.

transcript Your high school academic record. Your guidance counselor or registrar compiles this list of all your courses, grades, and standardized test scores. Your college will ask for official copies of your transcript. They should be signed across the seal by the appropriate school official and shouldn't be opened.

transfer Despite your best efforts, you may find that your chosen school isn't the perfect fit, or you may start out at junior college and decide that it's time to attend a four-year U. In either case, you may need to transfer to a different school. Transferring can be a tricky process, especially when it comes time to figure out how many of your previously earned credits will count at your new school. To make your transition as simple as possible, request application materials from prospective schools as early as possible and figure out how your credits will be accounted for before you apply.

U. Universities generally support both undergraduate and graduate programs and tend to be larger than colleges. You may find more research opportunities at a U., but you might get less attention from professors than at a college.

unsubsidized loans Unsubsidized loans are not need based, so all students are eligible to receive them. Interest payments begin immediately on unsubsidized loans, although you can waive the payments, and the interest will be capitalized.

walk-ons Usually unrecruited athletes who make the roster by proving themselves at open tryouts. This is difficult and depends on the school. Some schools rely on walk-ons to fill out their teams while others discourage walk-ons. Make sure you would be comfortable attending the school if you do not end up competing for the team.

weighted GPA Some high schools add 0.5 grade points to grades earned in AP or International Baccalaureate courses in order to reflect their unusual level of difficulty. If you have taken such courses, your GPA may be considered weighted. Some colleges convert weighted GPAs to standard GPAs for the purposes of comparison.

work-study An institutionally or federally funded employment program that provides students with part-time jobs—generally ten to fifteen hours per week.

Collegiate Athletics in Canada

If you are thinking of competing at the collegiate level in Canada, there's a few things you should know. In Canada, the Canadian Interuniversity Athletic Union (CIAU) is the equivalent of the NCAA. Regional champions from each of the five CIAU conferences compete at the CIAU National Championships each year.

In any given year, over ten thousand students athletes compete in three thousand events scheduled from September to March. The CIAU National Championships feature athletes in the following sports: soccer, cross-country, indoor track and field, field hockey, football, basketball, ice hockey, wrestling, swimming, and volleyball.

History

Founded in 1906, the original union existed until 1955. Then, it was only composed of universities in Ontario and Quebec. By 1955, the CIAU expanded to include nineteen universities in other provinces. Before total integration, individual provinces devised their own, unique athletic associations, following their own sets of rules. Finally, in the 1970s the CIAU was formed as a universal association for all of Canada.

Can a U.S. Resident Attend School in Canada?

Yes, however, admission rules vary for foreign students. Canadian universities do offer student-athlete financial assistance. The financial aid is not on the same scale as that of the United States, but Canadian colleges are cheaper than U.S. schools.

Before a student is given financial aid from a school, it has to be approved by the CIAU. Each year more than three hundred awards are offered to varsity athletes by universities across the country to assist in covering the cost of tuition. The amount of money varies; however, the award may not exceed $1,500 (Canadian dollars).

Canadians usually go to college in Canada, but there are some student-athletes who do come to U.S. schools and play sports on scholarship. However, there is no such thing as a full ride at a Canadian school. So, if you're an American student-athlete and you want to go to a Canadian school, call the coach before you make any financially based decisions. For more information about the CIAU, visit www.ciau.ca.

International Students

If you are an international student considering playing sports at an American U., you are not alone. Thousands of international students pursue a college athletic experience each year.

If you are not a U.S. citizen and you are interested in competing at the college level in the United States, then here is what you will need to do.

With thousands of college programs to choose from, you will need to get help from a good advisor.

If English is not your first language, then you will need to take the TOEFL (Test of English as a Foreign Language) or provide evidence that you are proficient in English. Most colleges and universities differ on the score needed for acceptance, but usually a score of 213 is suitable for the most prestigious schools in America.

You may also need to take the SAT or ACT. Most colleges and universities ask to see both the SAT and the TOEFL results of international student-athletes.

You should begin the recruitment and application process more than a year in advance. The earlier you start talking with coaches and admissions officers, the better your chances are of getting admitted and competing at the school of your choice.

You will need to obtain an I-20 Certificate of Eligibility from the school you plan to attend and also an F-1.

Review:
Ten Things to Remember during the Recruiting Process

Though there are many ways to attract a college coach's attention, if you make use of the following ten suggestions, you will be ahead of your competition:

1. **Succeed in the classroom.** You must achieve certain academic requirements to be eligible to play college sports. Don't let poor grades limit your choices. Strive for excellence!

2. **Keep an open mind.** Even if you have your heart set on one college team, keep your options open with a wide range of schools on your Target List.

3. **Promote yourself to college coaches.** Don't wait for coaches to find you. Call, write, or e-mail coaches to let them know that you want to play for their teams.

4. **Use all your resources.** Get your parents, high school coach, summer league coach, and guidance counselor involved in the recruiting process.

5. **Improve your entire package.** Good character, a positive attitude, a strong work ethic, and hustle are all important attributes that college coaches look for in players.

6. **Attend showcases, tournaments, and prospect camps.** These events are perfect opportunities to demonstrate your ability to many college coaches and pro scouts. They also let you see how you stack up with other players in your area.

7. **Explore all sources of financial aid.** Many students receive other sources of financial aid, not just athletic scholarships.

8. **Learn about all your options.** Become familiar with the different divisions and keep an open mind. Visit different campuses, use the Internet to research college websites, and ask questions. Remember, not only are you choosing a place to compete athletically, but you are selecting a new home.

9. **Set goals and deadlines.** Make lists of academic and athletic accomplishments that you want to achieve during each year of high school.

10. **Have fun.** Play for the love of the game.

How Did We Do?

Thank you for purchasing our *High School Athlete's Guide to College Sports*. Even though we are confident in our ability to help athletes like you navigate the recruiting process, we are always striving to improve. We would appreciate your input on what we can do to make this guide more educational for future readers.

Your name (optional): _____

Your e-mail address: _____

	Very	A lot	Somewhat	Not really	Not at all
How relevant was the guide's information?	☐	☐	☐	☐	☐
How thorough was the guide?	☐	☐	☐	☐	☐
How accurate was the guide's information?	☐	☐	☐	☐	☐
How easy was the guide to use?	☐	☐	☐	☐	☐
How appealing was the guide's design?	☐	☐	☐	☐	☐

What overall grade would you give the guide? (1–10, 10 being the best)

_____

What were the guide's strongest points?

_____

How could the guide be improved?

_____

Was there anything not in the guide that you wanted to know more about?

_____

Would you recommend this book to other athletes?　　☐ Yes　　☐ No

Other comments:

_____

_____

May we use your comments for promotional purposes?　　☐ Yes　　☐ No

Thank you for you help!

Please tear out this page and fax it to
(914) 232-2956, or mail it to:

College Bound Sports
60 Goldens Bridge Road
Katonah, NY 10536